PATRICK RODEN

Troubleshooting AGING

A Witty Guide to Getting Older and KICKING BUTT

Patrick Roden

Contents

Contents 3

Prologue 1

Introduction 4

1   Flip the Script on Aging 6

2   Aging Well Within One's Age (KISS) 20

3   The (SIMPLE) User Manual You Didn't Get 34

4   Ctrl+Alt+Delete Your Worries 53

5   Late Freedom: Don't Give a Sh*t 69

6   Lighten Your Load No One Wants Your Sh*t 83

7   Pushing Your Limits as You Age 95

8   Myth: Successful Aging is Ageless Aging 118

In Conclusion 137

Reference 138

About the Author 140

Also, by Patrick Roden 142

Prologue

Rethinking Aging (Seriously for a moment)

Lately, I've been reflecting on how fixed mindsets versus growth mindsets shape our perceptions of aging. The fixed mindset—still lingering from the 20th century—views aging through a lens of peaks and declines, a relic of the industrial era's obsession with productivity and efficiency. Back then, the dominant metaphor was "body-as- machine": a model that framed humans as having a few good years before inevitable breakdown.

This narrative wasn't just a product of cultural whimsy; it was deeply influenced by the medical model, which focused almost exclusively on pathology—what *goes wrong* as we age. This lens, rooted in ideas dating back to the ancient Greeks, gave us a narrow, decline-centered view of aging. It left little room to consider human growth, potential, or the possibility of thriving in later years. Tragically, even today, some cling to this outdated mindset, stuck in what feels like a low-grade form of gerontophobia: a fear of aging itself.

I'm not talking about "happy gerontology" where aging is viewed through the rose-colored glasses of denial, but rather choosing to emphasize a less gloomy ideal for growing older. Not "ageless aging" (impossibly aspirational; sorry Dick Clark) but aging well within one's age.

TROUBLESHOOTING AGING

Here's the irony—this fear of aging (aka Gerontophobia) is counter- productive not only for society but for our future selves. Aging isn't some external foe to be vanquished; it's the most natural process there is, a continuous journey of change (and human development) over time.

Time to Update Your Thinking

If the concept of aging makes you uncomfortable, pause for a moment. Why does it make you uneasy? Is it because you're still influenced by 20th-century prejudices you've unconsciously absorbed? Could you envision a vibrant, growth-oriented image of aging— one grounded in potential and continued development?

What makes thriving or living inherently better than aging? It's all about the perspective we choose to adopt. As we've seen with other "isms" throughout history, outdated cultural ideas erode not just our relevance but also our capacity to see the full humanity of others—and ourselves.

A New Vision for Aging

If we're going to create a 21st-century vision of aging, it starts by embracing the reality that aging is not a problem to solve but a process to engage with fully. Reframing aging as a natural, even empowering, process opens doors to new ways of thinking, living, and designing for our futures.

The opportunity is there, the question becomes, will we take it? If you're ready, READ ON!

Introduction

Aging often gets a bad rap. We hear complaints about creaky knees, laughing at gray hairs sprouting in odd places, and some grumblings about how today's pop music is lame compared to 70's ROCK (ok this is true). But here's the thing: aging isn't a glitch in the system— it's a feature. Just like your favorite tech device gets updates to improve its performance, aging is life's way of upgrading you, adding layers of experience, EARNED wisdom, and, let's face it, some really entertaining stories.

The problem isn't aging itself; it's how we've been conditioned to see it (we are aged by culture). We've been sold the myth that youth is the peak of life and everything after is just a long, slow decline (the old Peak & Decline theory of aging). But that's not reality...At least not mine and I'm willing to bet not entirely yours either. Aging is progression, not deterioration. It's about evolving, adapting, and thriving, even when things occasionally go off-script.

Think of this book as your troubleshooting guide for life's later stages—a manual for optimizing your "operating system" with humor, dignity— sorta, and a healthy dose of stubbornness. My goal is to reframe how you see aging, not as a problem to be fixed but as a challenge to embrace and an opportunity to kick a little butt along the way.

4

You've got the tools. You've got the attitude (*hell yeah*). Now, let's debug the myths about aging and get to work on creating your best possible vintage self— earned wrinkles, earned wisdom, and all.

Possibility Aging is Your Future,

Patrick Roden PhD

1

Flip the Script on Aging

It was formerly a terrifying view to me that I should one day be an old woman. I now find that Nature has provided pleasure for every state.

~ Mary Worley Montagu

Early in my nursing career, I had a moment that I now look back on as one of those "Aha!" experiences—except, it wasn't enlightening, it was hilarious. I was listening to the lungs of an elderly woman admitted with exacerbated congestive heart failure, a condition that often leads to repeat hospital visits. She was what we lovingly refer to as a "frequent flyer." This wasn't her first rodeo—no, she was a seasoned veteran of multiple acute episodes.

As I hurriedly placed my stethoscope in my ears, then strategically on her chest, I adopted my most professional "nurse voice" and said, "BIG BREATHS—BIG BREATHS!" (I'm sure you can imagine the authoritative tone.) Suddenly, she let out a chuckle and I could feel her whole body jiggle. Startled, I pulled one ear prong out to hear her better and asked, "What did you say?"

And then she hit me with it—straight out of the blue, in the most delightful Parkinson's-like voice you could imagine (think Katharine Hepburn in her golden years): "THEY USED TO BE..."

Beautiful young people are accidents of nature, but beautiful old people are works of art.

~ Eleanor Roosevelt

And just like that, her smirk and the twinkle in her eye turned an otherwise tense moment into a burst of shared laughter. Thirty years later, I still chuckle when I think about it. It wasn't just funny—it was a profound little moment of honesty about aging. Her lightheartedness taught me a lasting lesson: If we're fortunate enough to grow old, it would benefit us to accept the changes. But— *and here's the kicker*—we should do so with a touch of humor, just like she did.

I've shared this story many times, and it's always a crowd-pleaser. But it's more than just a funny story; it underscores a truth about aging. We often focus on the negatives: the sagging skin, the wrinkles, the failing memory—but there's so much more to it than that. Aging isn't a fate we have to *fight* against (anti-aging is anti-

7

living), it's an experience you create synergism with.

Further, I'll never forget an ad campaign by Kaiser Permanente that got it right. It was bold, brash, and brilliantly counter-cultural. The campaign asked, "DO YOU WANT TO BE AN OLD WOMAN?" Wait—what? Most companies are terrified to even utter the word "aging" or "old," but this one flipped the script. Instead of pushing chronic disease focus, Kaiser emphasized the importance of preventive care so you can live long enough to *become* an old woman! It was a refreshing message: don't fear getting old—embrace it!

Old people seem to be less in the business of creating things as creating selves.

~ W.M. Bortz, Dare *to be 100*

Aging, they said, isn't about decay; it's about making choices at every stage of life to live fully. It's about thriving, not surviving, and about being real with yourself. It's about rejecting the myth of "decline" and living vibrantly, no matter your age. Before you say that's sounds corny, there is some scientific proof.

Multiple studies over the past two decades show that individuals who maintain a positive outlook on aging tend to live longer and healthier lives than those with negative views about growing older. One such study,

8

published in *JAMA Network Open,* examined nearly 14,000 adults over the age of 50. It revealed that people with the highest satisfaction with aging had a 43% lower risk of dying from any cause over a four- year period compared to those who were least satisfied with the aging process.

Additionally, those with a more positive perspective on aging were less likely to develop chronic conditions such as diabetes, stroke, cancer, and heart disease. They also exhibited better cognitive functioning, engaged in more physical activity, and were less likely to experience sleep issues. Moreover, these individuals tended to have lower levels of loneliness, depression, and anxiety, while also exhibiting greater optimism and a stronger sense of purpose in life. The findings highlight the significant impact of mindset on both physical and mental health as we age.

This kind of humor helps me recall another woman who was quick- witted into her later years. Gypsy Rose Lee was a "stripper" (never fully undressed) and a towering intellect. She employed her craft to get men's attention as she mesmerized them into her way of thinking by political persuasion. She too could joke about her growing older and accepted herself at any age. For example, she once exclaimed:

I've got everything I always had. Only it's six inches lower!

So, go ahead and embrace aging with a confident, butt-kicking attitude! Don't buy into the fear and stigma surrounding aging—show the world you're not afraid to say the word "aging." Keep it real and embrace every stage with pride. After all, authenticity beats the latest miracle pill or Botox trend any day. Aging isn't about fighting change or pretending it isn't happening—it's about accepting it and striving to age well, whatever your age. And guess what? Science supports this mindset. Studies show that aging with a positive outlook and active engagement with life can significantly enhance your well-being and longevity. It's time to rewrite the narrative on aging—and you get to lead the charge!

They are anything but invisible

Why are we drawn to those who are a beautiful expression of aging? And when I say "we" I really am speaking for myself here–although it seems to be a shared experience. Whether it's in a cafe or a park walking the dog, encounters with mature women (focus on women for this) who are **aging well within their age** (not anti-aging), always have an allure; there is something about them.

Yes, it is cultural and subjective, but there is a certain something, an essence, it's almost palpable, a presence that appeals. A sense of self-assuredness, mature personal

10

style, and beingness that has been cultivated and forged over years of living and experience.

The quote **"We are aged by culture"** is attributed to Margaret Mead, an American cultural anthropologist. Mead knew aging is not just a physical phenomenon, but a cultural one too. In a youth-obsessed culture countless women can attest to this personally. Many women will also report that Life can be better with the passage of time in multiple ways, thanks to the advantages and opportunities that come with age (one of the aging paradoxes). This is where the scaffolding of that intangible essence of a beautiful expression of aging comes into play.

Elements of a Beautiful Expression of Aging

Here (in general terms) are the elements that inform that beautiful expression of aging:

Wisdom and Experience: Older women have accumulated a wealth of life experience, knowledge, and wisdom. They have had time to learn from successes and failures, which can lead to better decision-making and a more nuanced understanding of the world.

Personal Growth and Self-Acceptance: With age often comes a greater sense of self-acceptance and self-confidence. Older women may have a clearer understanding of their values, priorities, and strengths,

11

allowing them to embrace their authentic selves and live life on their own terms. **Strong Social Networks:** Older women tend to have well-established social networks built over the course of their lives. These networks can provide support, companionship, and opportunities for meaningful connections and shared experiences.

Increased Freedom and Independence: Many older women get a sense of liberation and freedom as they retire from work or have fewer caregiving responsibilities. This newfound freedom allows them to pursue hobbies, interests, and personal goals that may have been put on hold during earlier stages of life.

Opportunities for Reinvention and Exploration: Age can be a time of reinvention and exploration. Older women often can explore new passions, start new careers, travel, engage in volunteer work, or pursue higher education. This can bring a sense of fulfillment and excitement. **Emotional Well-being:** Older women may have developed coping mechanisms and emotional resilience over time. They may have a better ability to manage stress, adapt to challenges, and maintain emotional well-being. Research suggests that older adults generally experience higher levels of life satisfaction and happiness compared to younger age groups.

Intergenerational Relationships: Older women often have the opportunity to build meaningful relationships with younger generations, including grandchildren and extended family members. These relationships can bring joy, purpose, and a sense of continuity.

Advocacy and Empowerment: Older women have the potential to become advocates for issues they care about, using their voices and experiences to bring about positive change in their communities and society. This advocacy can contribute to a sense of purpose and make a difference in the world.

Confidence: Confidence is often seen as attractive at any age. Older women who exude self-assurance, embrace their life experiences, and feel comfortable in their own skin can be quite captivating.

Inner Beauty: Beauty goes beyond physical appearance. Older women who radiate kindness, compassion, and a positive outlook on life can be incredibly attractive. Inner beauty and a warm personality can be magnetic and draw people toward them.

Independence and Self-Sufficiency: Older women who are self- reliant, independent, and have a strong sense of personal identity can be very appealing. This shows strength, resilience, and the ability to navigate life on their own terms.

Style and Elegance: Older women often develop their

own unique sense of style over the years. Whether it's through fashion choices, grooming, or personal expression, a sophisticated and tasteful approach can be highly attractive.

Emotional Maturity: Emotional stability and the ability to communicate effectively are qualities that many people find attractive in older women. relationships with grace and understanding can be alluring.

Sense of Humor: Older women who have a playful and lighthearted attitude, who can laugh at themselves and enjoy life's moments, are often seen as attractive and enjoyable to be around.

Life Balance: Older women who have found a balance between their personal life, relationships, career, and self-care can be captivating. The ability to manage responsibilities and still prioritize personal well-being can be alluring to others.

Of course, It's important to note that some of these qualities are not exclusive to older women and can be attractive in people of all ages. Attractiveness is subjective and varies from person to person, so individual preferences may differ. It's essential to appreciate and value the uniqueness and beauty within every individual, regardless of age or gender. Yet, I find

14

qualities of this nature are more likely to be encountered in women past the age of 50.

Writer Mary Piper noted ***Somehow, I always felt that growing old happened to other people,*** and we soon find out it's a universal experience for those fortunate enough to reach fifty and beyond.

You are coming into your own, and you wear it well...

U-Shaped Happiness Curve

There is a robust body of research on getting older and happiness confirming yet another possible paradox of aging. Studies show that happiness peaks in your 20s, dips at middle age, and then begins to ascend once again after 50. When translated to a graph it appears in a "U" shape and has thus been dubbed the ***"U-Curve" of Happiness.***

An informative piece written by <u>Meg Selig in Psychology Today</u> un- packs several key elements to Happiness in old age:

1. Older Adults no longer require extraordinary experiences to be happy, rather they find happiness in ordinary things (aka mindfulness)
2. Meaningful relationships (authentic) are another source of hap- piness

15

3. Volunteering seems to be a common meme in the development of a happy old age
4. Purpose beyond the self is another

Happiness has been called a serious problem, and the pursuit of it is written into our very constitution making it an obsession in our country. The U-Curve of Happiness theory sounds like the kind of feel-good myth you'd hear at a wellness retreat. While it's backed by several studies and resonates with many, critics have emerged to poke holes in this sunny narrative, and they've got some compelling (and amusing) points.

The Happiness Curve May be More Turbulent

First up, the skeptics question the universality of the U-Curve. They point out that self-reported happiness can be influenced by culture, expectations, and even how the questions are asked. What counts as "happiness" in the United States might not align with definitions in Japan, Ghana, or even New Jersey. In some cultures, happiness isn't about feeling good all the time but about living a meaningful life—a sentiment that's hard to chart on a graph.

Next, there's the survivorship bias critique. Who's filling out these surveys? Mostly people who made it through midlife's stress tests with some optimism left intact. The grumpy or overwhelmed? They're likely too busy juggling bills and existential crises to answer questionnaires about their happiness levels.

Lastly, the critics point out that the "U" might just be a trick of our brains trying to make sense of randomness. Life isn't always a curve; sometimes, it's more of a roller coaster—or worse, a flat line.

Some argue that the U-Curve oversimplifies the complexities of aging, happiness, and individual differences. What about the person who peaks at 40 or finds bliss at 70 after discovering pickleball?

A Tentative Nod to the U-Shaped Curve

Still, in the United States, the U-Curve of Happiness does hold some water. Studies do suggest that many Americans rediscover contentment in later years, perhaps due to shifting priorities, fewer financial obligations, or simply letting go of societal pressures. The critics might raise valid questions, but the core idea—that happiness can rise as we age—is worth keeping in mind. After all, whether it's a U, a W, or just a hopeful squiggle, the curve gives us something to look forward to.

One more of my favorite stories about two "old women" and the power and wisdom that comes with aging—just to support my opening points here.

Two Old Women

In her book, Two Old Women: An Alaska Legend of
Betrayal, Courage and Survival

(1993), author Velma Wallis in the tradition of the keepers
of the stories, tells the Athabascan Indian legend passed
on from mothers to daughters of the upper Yukon River.

The story is about the nomadic people of the Gwich'in, who
belong to the Athabaska tribes that wandered the
territories of Yukon River, the Porcupine River, and the
Tanana Rivers. With the oncoming of a harsh winter and
lack of food, the tribe decides to leave behind two old women
in the snow-covered wilderness.

Abandoned and fearful, 75-year-old Sa' (means star) and
80-year-old Ch'idzigyaak (means chickadee bird) are left
with an elk's skin (gift of guilt) and a hatchet (gift of hope)
to die.

In desperation, they are faced with a choice point and decide
it is better to die trying to survive. First, the women kill a
squirrel using the hatchet, trap rabbits; each night, they dig
snow caves and save embers to renew each day's fire, so it
never goes out—and successfully hides from other
cannibalistic tribes. Over time they build up a generous
supply of foods and store them away.

18

The following winter, the weakened tribe returns to the area hungry and lacking to find the old women have not only survived but thrived. Over time the women forgive the tribe for abandoning them, and the group gains a new sense of survival.

From then on, the Gwich'in never leave their elderly behind. The tale is a beautiful message about the worth of older people (especially women) to society.

When Bob Dylan sang, *May you stay forever young*, that sounded like sage advice, but successful aging does not mean postponing aging; every stage of the process (orbit around the sun) has something to offer if lived fully within it. Stevie Nicks, in the song Landslide declared, *I'm getting older too,* and then asked: *Can I handle the seasons of my life?* and lately, it seems she seems to be doing it quite well.

Every age can be enchanting, provided you live within it.

~ Brigitte Bardot

Resource

TRUTH IN ME
I have no desire to fit in.
No plans
to walk with the crowd.
I have my own mind, heart

19

and soul. I am me and it
has taken me years to realize
how important that is.

~ R.M Drake

2

Aging Well Within One's Age (KISS)

When I get Old, they're never going to say, "What a sweet old lady." They're gonna say, "WHAT ON EARTH is she up to now"?!

~ Unknown

Keep It Simple Stupid

Aging well, living longer, and staying functional—it should be simple, right? But if you've tried to sift through the mountains of advice on how to age like a fine wine (or at least, not turn into a bottle of Mad Dog 2020), you know the struggle. In fact, getting reliable information about aging can feel like drinking from a firehose of TED Talks, podcast "biceps and concepts guys", tech billionaire bros are out there armed with unlimited funds to try and live forever— there's the latest crop of biohackers from Ivy League universities, discussing genetic mutations and cryonics like it's the latest hot dating trend. Trying to keep up with it all will age you! You've got companies selling "antioxidant" creams to boomers to fix turkey necks, PRejuvenation influencers selling anti-aging to preteens, apps designed to track your sleep cycles down to the nanosecond, and podcasts from hunky MD-types who

21

author the latest best sellers on the science of longevity. The target audiences of anxious hyper fit millennials struggling to adhere to complex regimes mere mortals find impossible, all in the hopes of a future promise of "super-aging." It's exhausting, just trying to figure out where to start.

But why does it have to be so complicated to age well? I'd like to propose a simple solution—no more firehose of information, no more trying to fit into a one-size-fits-all blueprint. Instead, let's take a page from an old-school engineering principle and keep it simple, stupid (KISS).

KISS: Simplicity is the Ultimate Sophistication

You've probably heard the acronym KISS tossed around in various contexts—mostly when someone's struggling with a complicated process that could have been simpler. But KISS isn't just a pithy joke; it's a tried-and-true principle that's been around since the 1960s, coined by Kelly Johnson, the head engineer at Lockheed Skunk Works (basically, the cool kids' club of airplane development). The KISS principle has been applied in everything from software to product design, and it's as relevant today in aging as it was in aviation.

The idea is simple: keep things as uncomplicated as possible. Because, let's face it, the more complicated we make things, the less likely we are to stick with them. It's like buying a gym membership with the best intentions, only to be overwhelmed by all the machines and end up on the elliptical staring at the ceiling wondering what the heck you're doing there.

The 3-Legged Stool of Aging Well

So, let's break aging well down into three simple legs. Yes, I said "legs"—because, quite frankly, we all need them to keep moving.

Leg One: Leg Strength and Mortality Rates

This might sound like a no-brainier, but it's critical. Research shows that people with greater leg strength have a lower risk of mortality. In other words, if you can squat down to pick up a pencil without grunting like you're lifting a refrigerator, you're already ahead of the game. Strength in your legs can improve balance, mobility, and help prevent falls (which, let's face it, can be dangerous and steal dreams). So, simple action step here: get on a leg strengthening program (the one below is just a suggestion—there are many on YouTube). Consult with your doctor or physical therapist first but make it a priority. Even just a few squats a day can be a game-changer.

Example of simple leg strengthening exercise you can do at home

Lower Body Strengthening Exercises for Seniors

1. **Sit to Stand**
   - **Description:** Practice moving from sitting to standing without using your hands.
   - **Benefits:** Strengthens hips and legs, crucial for maintaining physical independence and confidence.
2. **Heel Stand**
   - **Description:** Lift your toes while keeping your heels on the ground.
   - **Benefits:** Strengthens front lower leg muscles, improves balance, and helps prevent tripping.
3. **Ankle Circles**
   - **Description:** Rotate your ankles in circles while seated or standing.
   - **Benefits:** Enhances ankle flexibility, crucial for stability as well as mobility.
4. **Hip Marching**
   - **Description:** While seated, lift knees alternately in a marching motion.
   - **Benefits:** Strengthens hip flexors and thighs, promotes core stability with correct posture.
5. **Side Hip Raise**
   - **Description:** Stand and raise one leg sideways, then return to the starting position.
   - **Benefits:** Strengthens side hip muscles, helpful for hip arthritis and lateral movement.
6. **Calf Raises**

- **Description:** Lift heels off the ground while standing, then lower slowly.
- **Benefits:** Strengthens calves, improves blood circulation, and boosts walking power.

7. **Knee Extension**
   - **Description:** Extend one leg straight out while seated, then lower it slowly.
   - **Benefits:** Strengthens knees, improves range of motion, and aids balance.

8. **Partial Squats**
   - **Description:** Perform shallow squats with support if needed.
   - **Benefits:** Increases hip flexibility and quadriceps strength, improves ability to rise from a chair.

9. **Hip Extension**
   - **Description:** Extend one leg backward while standing, holding onto a chair for support.
   - **Benefits:** Strengthens hip joints, enhances walking and stair- climbing ability.

10. **Standing Knee Flexion**
    - **Description:** Bend one knee backward while standing, bringing your heel toward your buttocks.
    - **Benefits:** Strengthens hamstrings and improves standing balance.

11. **Lunges**
    - **Description:** Step forward into a lunge position, lowering your back knee slightly.
    - **Benefits:** Strengthens quadriceps and hips, aids

with balance and household lifting tasks.

12. **Straight Leg Raise**

- **Description:** While lying down, raise one leg straight up and lower it slowly.
- **Benefits:** Builds quadriceps and hip flexor strength, assists with **walking and core stability.**

How often to do them?

Exercise Guidelines:

- **Frequency:** Aim for **2-3 times per week**.
- **Duration:** Perform each exercise for **10-15 minutes** per session.
- **Repetitions:** Start with **8-12 repetitions** for each exercise and gradually increase as you become comfortable.
- **Sets:** Perform **1-2 sets** of each exercise, resting between sets.

Additional Tips:

- **Warm-Up:** Begin with gentle movements like ankle circles or light marching for 3-5 minutes.
- **Rest Days:** Ensure at least one rest day between sessions to allow for recovery.
- **Listen to Your Body:** Adjust intensity based on comfort and avoid overexertion.

Weekly Example Schedule:

- **Monday:** Sit to Stand, Calf Raises, Knee Extension
- **Wednesday:** Side Hip Raise, Hip Marching, Heel Stand
- **Friday:** Partial Squats, Hip Extension, Lunges

This routine helps build strength, balance, and mobility safely over time.

Note: ALWAYS consult your healthcare provider before embarking on this, or any exercise program (read that again!).

Leg Two: Daily Novelty and Complexity

What does "novelty" mean in aging? It's not about jumping out of an airplane (unless that's your thing), but about engaging with the world in a way that keeps your brain firing on all cylinders (dendrites and brain cells-neurons). Studies show that environmental complexity— the variety in your daily life—can boost neurogenesis, the growth of new neurons and connections called dendrites. So, mix things up! Take a different route to work, try a new recipe, sign up for that dance class.

The more new experiences you expose yourself to, the more your brain will thank you. The simple action step: Build newness into your day, every day. You'll not only keep your brain sharp, but you might even discover that you like sushi (or at least, that groovy local jazz bar).

Routines are comforting, and yes, we love them by default but be purposeful in doing something new to you each week.

"When you expose your brain to an environment that's novel and complex or new and difficult, the brain literally reacts. Those new and challenging situations cause the brain to sprout dendrites (dangling extensions) which grow the brain's capacity."

~ Dr. Paul D. Nussbaum, Clinical neuropsychologist
University of Pittsburgh

Further, ever take a trip and feel "refreshed" after? When you travel, you are constantly challenged to solve issues, negotiate different languages at times, meet new people, deal with exchange rates, find lost luggage (hate that), and try new foods (love that)—to mention only a few.

Dr. Nussbaum also suggests travel as a way to not just preserve brain function into old age, but to actually stimulate a specific kind of brain growth.

Paul Nussbaum, **traveling can stimulate your brain and encourage the growth of new connections within cerebral matter.** *The key concept is the link between new experiences and the generation of dendrites within the* *brain.*

Dendrites are branch-like extensions that grow from brain neurons. Their role is to facilitate the transmission of information between different regions of the brain. In brief, the greater your number of functioning dendrites, the better your brain will perform. This aids in maintaining cognitive functions such as memory and attention.

Nussbaum points out that when you travel to a new location, your brain is forced to make sense of new stimuli. This triggers the production of new dendrites. In Nussbaum's words, your brain "literally begins to look like a jungle."

Source: lifehack.org

Good News: So, the reason you feel "refreshed" in part is due to fact that all the novelty and complexity has stimulated new dendrites and neurons. You literally have a different brain at the end of your trip, it's been rewired, kind of...

Bad News: Chronic Stress can undo all that lovely rewiring. I'll be brief here and stay out of the weeds, but it's well-established stress can trim out dendrites (those connections between brain neurons) like a weed- wacker in the hands of a caffeinated teenager.

Chronic stress can also have specific negative effects on brain tissue and function. Persistently high levels of glucocorticoids inhibit neuron growth inside the hippocampus, impairing the normal processes of memory formation and recall. Stress hormones can also suppress neural pathways that are normally active in decision-making and cognition, and accelerate the deterioration in brain function caused by aging.

~ Source: brainfacts.org

Leg Three: We Are Aged by Culture—But Only If We Agree to It

Here's a biggie: culture. Western society has this peculiar habit of shoving ageism down our throats, like some bad reality TV show we can't escape from. "Get old, get irrelevant," they say (become invisible). But you don't have to buy into that narrative. Don't let society tell you that aging means slowing down, fading into the background, or becoming irrelevant. You're never too old to break the mold. Whether it's learning a new skill, running a marathon, or starting a business, you get to decide how you age. So, the action step is simple: reject the cultural narrative of ageism, and lead by example.

Age Beliefs

"In Japan, it became clear to me that the culture we're in

impacts how we age."

~ Becca Levy PhD

Shortly after her death, I made a surprising discovery. While analyzing data from my study about the lives and outlooks of the inhabitants of the small town of Oxford, Ohio, I found out that the single most important factor in determining the longevity of these inhabitants — more important than gender, income, social background, loneliness, or functional health — was how people thought about and approached the idea of old age. Age beliefs, it turns out, can steal or add nearly eight years to your life. In other words, these beliefs don't just live in our heads. For better or worse, those mental images that are the product of our cultural diets, whether it's the shows we watch, the things we read, or the jokes we laugh at, become scripts we end up acting out.

~ *Excerpted from* "Breaking the Age Code: How Your Beliefs About Aging*

Determine How Long & Well You Live"* *by Becca Levy* Bottom line, how you view your aging, beyond what the culture thinks about it, is key to getting older and kicking butt—be unstoppable!!

A Note from the Author (me): Why KISS Works (Even If It's Too Simple) Okay, okay. I can already hear some of you saying, "This sounds *too* simple. Where's the fancy science, the Blue Zones diets and cutting-edge exercise research?" I can just hear it... "This guy's a light weight!"

I get it. As someone who's spent plenty of time buried in the latest longevity studies, I know there's a lot of *complicated* stuff out there. But here's the thing: when it comes to making decisions about how to age well, too many choices can be overwhelming. It's called "overchoice," and it's a real cognitive killer. How do I know this you might ask? Well, thirty-five plus years in the trenches of hands-on caring for real people, many in their later years, you learn a thing or two. Like what works— what doesn't.

Too much complexity is a barrier for many, myself included. I'm for keeping it simple. When given too many complex options, the tendency can be not deciding at all— or worse, regretting the one made and going in the opposite direction.

That's why KISS is practical and effective—it strips away most of the unnecessary complexity and gives you just enough to make practical, sustainable choices.

This 3-legged stool of aging well is like a climber's toehold, it's a place to start to reach higher ground. So, there you have it. The three simple legs of aging well, with a dash of humor and a lot of science to back them up. Keep it simple, stay strong, embrace novelty, and reject ageism. Aging isn't a bug in the system; it's just another phase of life that we can live well—without the stress of trying to be forever young (sorry Bob Dylan). KISS it, and you might just find that functional aging is simpler (and more fun) than you ever imagined.

Summary / Review

I suggested the 3-legged stool for aging well concept and keeping it simple. Leonardo da Vinci was credited with stating: **"simplicity is the ultimate sophistication."** So, in that spirit let's look at the key points of this chapter:

1) Keep Your Legs Strong (do the exercises). This one is the biggest bang for your buck.

2) Keep Novelty and Complexity in your daily behaviors (try something new). Travel, your brain will love you for it! No matter how small, just do it (thanks, Nike).

3) Reject Negative Cultural Assumptions About Aging— your culture or your neighbor's ageism is none of your business (F*ck them).

So, get these 3 down first and if you want to add more later (diet, more exercise, purpose, etc...keep reading)—but start with these for now.

Resources (Peer Review Science) Serious sh*t

Hill, J. (2017, February 11). Neuroscientist says when you travel, your brain reacts in a special way. *Lifehack.* https://www.lifehack.org/53647 8/neuroscientist-says-when-you-travel-your-brain-reacts-special- way

Levy, B. (2022, August 10). How America's ageism hurts, shortens lives of elderly. *Harvard Gazette.* https://news.harvard.edu/gazette/story/ 2022/08/how-americas-ageism-hurts-shortens-lives-of-elderly/

Nussbaum, P. D. (n.d.). How travel stimulates brain growth. *Lifehack.* https://www.lifehack.org/articles/lifestyle/how-travel-stimulates-brai n-growth.html

O'Neill, M. (2024, November 7). A 30-second balance test can indicate how well you're aging, study shows. *Verywell Health.* https://www.very wellhealth.com/30-second-balance-test-aging-7428768

See

A 30-Second Balance Test Can Indicate How Well YOu're Aging, Study Shows by Maggie O'Neill / Published on November 07, 2024, Found veryhealth.com

Hill, J. (2017, February 11). Neuroscientist says when you travel, your brain reacts in a special way. Lifehack. https://www.lifehack.org/53647 8/neuroscientist-says-when-you-travel-your-brain-reacts-special- way

3

The (SIMPLE) User Manual You Didn't Get

It's been said, your biography becomes your biology.

~ Unknown

When the Warning Light Comes On

Ah, turning 50ish plus. It's like discovering that your body has been running on an outdated operating system, and suddenly, those software updates are no longer optional. Yes, you partied back in the day and now that check engine light keeps coming on. You can ignore it, put a piece of black electrical tape over it, or start some overdue repairs.

Welcome to the "Version 5.0ish" of you—complete with unexpected pop-ups, AARP solicitations, slower processing speeds, and error messages that say, "Why did I walk into this room again?"

The line: "If I had known I was going to live this long I would have taken better care of myself," has been attributed to several people— I'm going with Mickey Mantel. Time to take his advice and do a little maintenance (before it's last of the 9th inning and there are two out and you're not ahead). Well, consider this chapter your overdue trou- bleshooting guide covering the big two factors (but not too obnoxiously complex), eating and moving for longevity (aka diet and exercise). I'll keep it simple (KISS).

The Longevity Diet: Upgrade Your Body's Operating System

- Why your metabolism is suddenly running in "safe mode."
- The ultimate guide to fueling your body for energy, vitality, and longevity (and enjoying food without calorie-counting madness).

Fuel Your Longevity (Nothing too Crazy)

The key to a long, healthy life? A well-rounded, plant-packed diet that includes lots of fruits, vegetables, nuts, legumes, and whole grains. Simple enough, right? But here's the kicker—avoiding the bad stuff is just as important! We're talking added sugars, sodium, and saturated fats, which are all the wrong kinds of guests at your longevity party.

Of course, your genes are a factor, but don't blame them entirely for how long you'll stick around. Studies suggest that around 25% of your longevity is determined by your genetic code, while the rest is up to your lifestyle choices, including diet and exercise. So, if you're gunning for those extra years, what you eat matters—a lot.

Metabolism in "Safe Mode" (the Basics)

Ah, aging metabolism—nature's way of saying, *"Remember when you could eat a whole pizza without consequences? Well, enjoy your salad!"* But why does your body suddenly act like a calorie-hoarding dragon? Let's break it down:

Metabolism naturally slows with age due to a combination of physio- logical, hormonal, and lifestyle factors:

1. Loss of Muscle Mass (Sarcopenia)

Muscles are your body's calorie-burning MVPs, and they slowly leave the building after age 30. Why? They probably got tired of your shenanigans. Less muscle means fewer calories burned, even when you're binge- watching TV. Solution? Start lifting—weights, groceries, or even your dog. Whatever works, aka resistance training.

Muscle tissue burns more calories than fat, even at rest. As we age, we naturally lose muscle mass—starting around age 30 as mentioned, we lose about 3-8% per decade, and this accelerates after 60. Less muscle means a lower resting metabolic rate (RMR), the number of calories burned while the body is at rest.

2. Hormonal Changes

Remember those energetic hormones from your youth? They've retired to Florida (Johnathan Winters called FL God's waiting room). As testosterone and estrogen levels drop, so does your metabolic hustle. Plus, your thyroid might get a little *lazy*. Time for some gentle encouragement: exercise, sleep, and maybe fewer donuts...

Hormones that regulate metabolism, such as testosterone in men and estrogen in women, decline with age. This decrease contributes to muscle loss and fat gain, slowing down the metabolic rate. Thyroid function can also decline, reducing metabolic efficiency.

3. Decreased Physical Activity

Let's face it: the older some of us get, the more we value *"sit-down"* activities—like scrolling through streaming options. Less activity equals fewer calories burned. So, find something fun that makes you move! Dance around the house, chase your grandkids, or walk your imaginary (actually, get a shelter dog) dog. Just don't be still. The motivation guru, Tony Robbins once quipped; "Motion equals emotion," I love that!

Many people become less active with age, leading to

reduced energy expenditure and muscle loss. Lower activity levels mean fewer calories burned daily, contributing to a slower metabolism.

4. Reduced Mitochondrial Efficiency

Your mitochondria, aka cellular powerhouses, are like tiny engines that lose horsepower over time. They burn fuel less efficiently, which means your body converts food into "nap time" rather than energy.

These Powerhouses of cells that generate energy, over time, become less and less efficient and numerous as we age. This decline affects how effectively the body converts food into energy, slowing overall metabolism. Fuel them with protein and exercise—they love it.

5. Changes in Fat Distribution

Ever notice how fat migrates to new neighborhoods as you age? It loves settling around your organs (visceral fat), and it doesn't burn many calories. Think of it as a bad roommate that never pays rent. This shift reduces the overall metabolic rate. Evict it with strength training and good nutrition!

Did you know that the average weight of a bowling ball typically ranges from 10 to 14 pounds for beginners and 14 to 16 pounds for experienced players? Let's say you'd like to lose 30 lbs., which means you're carrying around the equivalent of TWO BOWLING BALLS everywhere you go! Image what that does to your energy level, your cardiovascular level, and your skeletal system?!

Being only 10 pounds overweight increases the force on the knee by 30-60 pounds with each step.

~ Johns Hopkins Arthritis Center

6. Cellular Aging

As cells age, processes like protein synthesis and energy production become less efficient. Cellular repair slows, reducing overall metabolic function. Your metabolism isn't broken; it's just a little lonely. Treat it well with movement, muscle-building, and good food. You might not be able to *out-pizza* your younger self anymore, but with a little effort, you can still outlast them on the dance floor.

Combatting Metabolic Slowdown

While aging is inevitable (if you're lucky), lifestyle choices can mitigate metabolic decline:

- **Strength Training**: Building or maintaining muscle mass can counteract metabolic slowdown.
- **Staying Active**: Regular aerobic and resistance exercises help keep metabolism active.
- **Protein Intake**: Adequate protein supports muscle

maintenance and repair.

- **Hydration and Sleep**: Both are crucial for optimal metabolic func- tion.

How Food Impacts Longevity (Not Rocket Science and You've Heard it All Before)

A diet packed with the good stuff—think fruits, veggies, nuts, and legumes—can reduce your risk of death from various diseases like cancer, heart disease, and neurodegenerative conditions. Research supports this: a massive 2023 study that tracked the eating habits of over 120,000 people for 30 years found that those who ate these longevity- boosting foods were less likely to die prematurely.

These nutrient-dense foods are like a supercharged multivitamin, providing antioxidants, fiber, and essential minerals that support overall health, keep your weight in check, and ward off diseases.

Vegetables and Fruits: The MVPs of Longevity

Getting your five servings of fruits and veggies a day is one of the easiest ways to add years to your life. But here's the truth: most Americans are way behind. Only about 10% of U.S. adults meet the daily veggie requirement, and only 12% hit the target for fruit. So, let's step up our game!

Studies show that people who consume more fruits and vegetables are at a lower risk for heart disease, cancer, and other chronic conditions. Aim for at least five servings a day—and don't worry, more veggies and fruit will only make your future self-happier (though hitting five seems to be the sweet spot).

Tips for Eating More Produce:

- Add fresh fruit to salads or stir-fries for a burst of flavor.
- Make a smoothie with greens and frozen berries.
- Get into the habit of adding a cup of fruit to breakfast and a second as a snack.

Nuts: Tiny Powerhouses for Big Health Benefits

Nuts are like little nutritional superheroes: full of healthy fats, protein, fiber, and antioxidants. They're not just great for snacking, either—regular consumption has been linked to improved metabolic markers (goodbye, waistline) and a reduced risk of chronic disease. A study found that eating more nuts helped people with metabolic syndrome lower their triglyceride levels and improve cholesterol.

How to Add More Nuts to Your Diet:

- Toss nuts into your salads, stir-fries, or baked goods.

- Use nut butter as a dip for fruits or as a spread on toast.
- Blend them into smoothies for a protein boost.

Meat-Free Meals for More Life

Cutting back on red and processed meat might just be your ticket to a longer, healthier life. Think of it as giving your arteries a vacation and your heart a well-deserved break. Research shows that reducing meat—even a few days a week—can dramatically lower your risk of heart disease and boost life expectancy. If you need inspiration, look no further than the folks in Okinawa, Japan, or Ikaria, Greece. These "Blue Zones" are home to some of the world's happiest centenarians, and their secret? Mostly plants. (And probably not wondering, "Is bacon a vegetable?").

Plant-Based Swaps You Won't Hate:

Bean-based chili: All the flavor, none of the mooo.

Lentil stew: Like a warm hug that's also fighting for your longevity.

Hummus and veggies: Your new snack buddy—sorry, processed meats, you're out of the club. Remember: In a world where bacon seems to go with everything, be the person who pairs hummus with joy.

44

Mediterranean Diet: The Gold Standard for Longevity

The Mediterranean diet is often hailed as one of the best for health and longevity. It emphasizes fruits, vegetables, whole grains, nuts, and healthy fats, with moderate consumption of seafood, dairy, and even wine! Plus, it limits meat and sweets—two things that don't have a long shelf life in a healthy diet.

A study in 2014 (not new information) linked adherence to the Mediterranean diet with longer telomeres (the caps on our chromosomes that protect our DNA). Longer telomeres mean a longer, healthier life. So, the Mediterranean diet doesn't just help you feel good—it might just help you live longer.

How to Eat Mediterranean-Style:

- Make simple meals like fish with roasted veggies, quinoa, and olive oil.
- Use olive oil instead of butter for cooking.
- Snack on fresh fruit, nuts, and olives.

Green Tea: A Sip Toward Longevity

Can drinking green tea really add years to your life? While the jury's still out, studies suggest that regular green tea drinkers are at a lower risk for heart disease, stroke, and certain cancers. So, why not swap your regular cup of coffee for green tea and enjoy its potential health benefits?

How to Drink Green Tea:

- Sip matcha in the morning for an extra boost.
- Add green tea to smoothies, oatmeal, or even soups and stews.
- Just remember to cut off caffeine by late afternoon to avoid disturbing your beauty sleep.

What to Avoid for Longevity

No one's saying you can never indulge, but certain foods should be limited if you're serious about aging well. Here's what to keep in moderation:

- Added sugars (cakes, cookies, sodas)
- Processed and red meats
- High-sodium snacks
- Saturated fats (like butter, cheese, and palm oil)

In the end, if you want to live a long, happy life, it's all about balance. Keep the fruits and veggies coming, ditch the processed junk, and don't forget to move your body—exercise is just as important as diet for longevity. Plus, it's never too late to start! So, here's to living longer and feeling better.

Source: Best Diet for Longevity: What To Eat and Avoid

System Updates: Exercise

- Getting your body back online through movement.
- How to optimize your muscle strength, bone health, and flexibility— without crash dieting or marathon workouts.

For a longevity-boosting workout, you don't have to train like an Olympic athlete or squeeze into those teeny-tiny leggings. Research suggests that simple movements—yes, even as little as 15 minutes a day— can lead to significant health benefits, improving strength, flexibility, and even cognitive function. Here's how you can get your body moving for longevity:

1. **Chair and Wall Yoga**: These simple yet effective practices are excellent for seniors or anyone new to movement. They can enhance flexibility, improve balance, and even boost mood. Chair yoga allows you to engage in stretches while seated, perfect for building muscle and improving mobility without stress on your joints

Good Resource: California Mobility 21 Chair Exercises for Seniors: Complete Visual Guide (californiamobility.com)

1. **Feldenkrais Method**: This approach focuses on gentle, mindful movements designed to improve body awareness and function. It helps with everything from improving

posture to reducing pain and stiffness, making it an ideal low-impact exercise

Good Resource: The Feldenkrais Project: Donor-Supported Feldenkrais Lessons for All! (feldenkraisproject.com)

Weight Resistance Training: Contrary to what you might think, lifting weights isn't just for bodybuilders. Sensible, low-intensity weight training can help preserve bone density, prevent age-related muscle loss, and even support heart health. Studies show that even short, daily sessions of weight resistance (as little as 15 minutes) can yield noticeable benefits

Good Resource: California Mobility 21 Chair Exercises for Seniors: Complete Visual Guide

In short, just 15 minutes a day of mindful movement—whether through chair yoga, Feldenkrais, or resistance training—can be a game changer for your longevity. Not only do you get stronger, but you're also investing in a body that's more flexible, balanced, and ready for whatever comes next.

Remember, you can take the time to be healthy—or you can take the time to be sick.

Final Thoughts on Exercise and Longevity—Get a Shelter Dog

Want to add years to your life, and life to your years? Get a dog—and better yet, adopt a shelter pet! It turns out, the secret to a longer, happier life might just be wagging its tail and begging for belly rubs.

Studies show that dog owners are *more* likely to get active—and we're not just talking about chasing after them when they steal your sandwich. Walking your dog counts as exercise, even if they're just sauntering along, tail in the air like they own the neighborhood. One study found that dog owners are more likely to meet daily physical activity recommendations (say goodbye to sedentary lifestyle blues) It's basically nature's stress-relief therapy, no co-pay required. And if you get your dog from a shelter, you're also saving a life. Win-win!

As for the perks of adopting from a shelter, they're endless. Not only are you rescuing a pet, but you're also getting an *instant* workout partner, personal stress therapist, and a furry companion to keep you on your toes (literally). Oh, and if you're feeling lonely, nothing beats the unconditional companionship of a shelter pup—or two, or three, no judgment here! You'll feel like a superhero while simultaneously getting the ultimate loyalty squad.

So, why not head over to your local shelter? Your future dog (and your future self) will thank you. They might even give you a high-five—okay, a paw, but it counts in my longevity book!

"On Successful Aging" (Going to Get serious but Just for a Moment)

I recently read a comment in response to the concept of "Successful Aging." The individual questioned the term/idea of successful aging. They asked "What does successful aging even mean? A fair question and one that was addressed decades ago.

In 1999, I read one of the most influential books on aging that shaped much of my thinking on the topic. The book was titled, *SCCCESSFUL AGING*, it was written by John Wallis Rowe M.D., and Robert L. Kahn. PhD. I referenced the work in many talks, papers, and conversations in the early days of my gerontological journey.

The book questioned historic gerontology and the Peak-Decline medical model of aging—really for the first time in mass media. It was bold in content and dared to explore aspects of aging that went well (free of pathology). **The authors employed scientific rigor and used the theoretical scaffolding The MacArthur Foundation studies** (longitudinal research) to show empirically that human development was possible in the later stages of life.

It was beyond happy talk about getting old (Happy Gerontology) and was the foundational work for much the current trend of viewing aging from a critical perspective of questioning cultural assumptions about aging (ageism).

So called Successful Aging is multidimensional and according to Rowe and Kahn, consists of the following elements:

- **Avoiding disease and disability**
- **Having high cognitive, mental and physical function**
- **Being actively engage in life**
- **Being psychologically well adapted in later life**

These defining components have themselves aged well, and in my opinion remain a solid definition of aging successfully (more on these to come).

Now, having covered all this, I feel compelled to share a passage from one of my favorite books on aging; WOMEN ROWING NORTH: Navigating Life's Currents and Flourishing as We Age, by Mary Pipher (2019). Pipher notes:

Unless carefully managed, a physical disability can become a social and emotional one. I didn't want to spend my life maintaining my health—I wanted to be fully alive and engaged with the world. I asked myself, "How much of my time should I spend doing things that are good for me? And how much time should I save to do things that are important to me?

A good question to ask of one's self—those don't

necessarily have to be mutually exclusive, but getting older and kicking butt means more than anxiously trying hard not to die.

Summary Message

OK, not going to get preachy, we're all adults here. . .Longevity doesn't need to be rocket science. My Aunt Ann lived to 96, worked all her life, retired from her job at 90 (they downsized her, and she wanted to sue for age-discrimination), lived a full rich life until the end. She exercised daily (YMCA classes after work), volunteered in her community (donated 90 GALLONS of blood to the Red Cross in her lifetime), loved the outdoors, was a reader, pet owner, and a happy woman who enjoyed a glass of wine (or two) on the weekends, at sensibly, laughed easily, was grateful and loved life (she did have a 68' Mustang too).

No fancy diets, no anti-aging snake oil, no Botox, no fasting, no expensive supplements, no early retirement to Florida or elaborate assisted living facilities—she was always ready for an adventure, big or small, and was a delight to be around. She knew how age well within her age. She kept it simple.

References/ Resources (serious sh*t)

Hu, F. B., Song, M., & Zhong, J. (2014). Mediterranean diet

and telomere length in Nurses' Health Study: Population-based cohort study. *BMJ*, 349, g6674. https://doi.org/10.1136/bmj.g6674

Johns Hopkins Arthritis Center. (n.d.). *Role of body weight in os- teoarthritis.* Johns Hopkins Arthritis Center. Retrieved November 24, 2024, from

https://www.hopkinsarthritis.org/patient-corner/disease-   management/role-of-body-weight-in-osteoarthritis/

Longo, V. (2022, April 28). New article outlines the characteristics of a "Longevity Diet". University of Southern California, Leonard Davis School of Gerontology. https://gero.usc.edu/2022/04/28/valter-longo- longevity-diet/

Rowe, J. W., & Kahn, R. L. (1999). *Successful aging.* Pantheon Books. Sass, C. (2024, June 19). *What to eat to help you live longer and healthier.*

Health. Retrieved from https://www.health.com/nutrition/longevity- diet

While the 2018 physical activity guidelines recommend that adults engage in at least 150 to 300 minutes per week of moderate exercise, 75 to 150 minutes each week of vigorous movement or an equivalent combination of both intensities, it turns out that if adults do more than the recommended amount, it can lower their risk of death. Moderate physical activity is defined as walking, weightlifting and lower-intensity exercise. Meanwhile, vigorous exercise is categorized as running, bicycling and swimming *(Massive study uncovers how much exercise is needed to live longer | American Medical Association)*.

10 Science-Based Benefits of Having a Dog

Owning a dog can help you live longer. A comprehensive review of studies published between 1950 and 2019 found that dog owners had a lower risk of death. Studies suggest that dog owners have lower blood pressure levels and improved responses to stress. Research has concluded that the bond between humans and dogs reduces stress, which is a major cause of cardiovascular problems.

Source: 10 Benefits of Having a Dog, According to Scientific Research

Author Note: Always check with your doctor first before starting an exercise program.

KISS (EAT < MOVE)

4

Ctrl+Alt+Delete Your Worries

Curiosity, discovery, creativity, and imagination are essential qualities in life, especially for children." ~
Excerpt from a writers' newsletter

Learn. UnLearn. ReLearn.

The opening sentence above was part of an Author's newsletter I received. As I read it recently, I certainly agreed with it, but not being focused on children's books my thoughts immediately went to older adults.

Why are these qualities atrophied with age for so many, and yet retained by others? The law of familiarity certainly plays a role, and my argument is these qualities are no less essential for older adults— and in fact are even more remarkable in individuals with more water under the bridge (aging and experience).

"Beginner's mind" and suspension of "been there done that" are superpowers of older creative types.

According to Susan David (see susandavid.com), a top

psychologist in the field of emotional agility, there are two ways to think about life as you age: the **fixed mindset** and the **growth mindset**. Let's start with the fixed mindset—the kind of thinking that says, "I'm too old to learn how to use TikTok" or "I've been this way for decades, why change now?"

For those with a fixed mindset, aging means a slow, inevitable slide (the old Peak and Decline Model) into becoming the cranky neighbor who yells at kids to get off the lawn—and that's *if* you're lucky enough to still have a lawn!

The fixed mindset is rooted in the belief that our abilities, like our memory or energy levels, are set in stone, and we can't really improve or change them. If you think the aging process means you're stuck with whatever mental glitches or aches you've got, you might be riding the fixed mindset train straight to the "too old for this" station.

Now, let's talk about the **growth mindset**—the kind of thinking that says, "You know what? I may not be able to remember where I put my keys, but I can still learn how to meditate to calm my mind." According to Susan David, adopting a growth mindset means believing that you can always improve and learn, no matter how many candles are on your birthday cake. People with a growth mindset approach aging like it's a new season of a show they love sure, the plot's different, but it's still an opportunity to see what happens next. Want to take up a new hobby? Go for it. Trying to remember your Wi-Fi password for the 100th time this week? You've got this. The growth mindset doesn't say "I'm too old to start something new"; it says, "Okay, let's try and if I fail, I'll just call it 'part of the learning process.'"

David's research shows that people with a growth mindset are way more adaptable, and that's key as we age. They see emotional bumps, memory lapses, or even stress as things to work through, not as signs of "you've reached your expiration date." So, instead of worrying about getting older, they tackle challenges head-on, saying things like, "Okay, so I can't remember where I put my glasses—but maybe I'll find them in the next room while I take a nap, and in the meantime, I'll enjoy the process!" That's emotional agility at its finest.

In other words, the growth mindset tells you: It's never too late to try again, and it's definitely never too late to laugh about it while you're at it. And if you can't find the glasses? Just turn it into an impromptu nature walk (because who doesn't love a good "I'll find it later" stroll?)

"Forest Bathing" The Science of Awe: Nature's Prescription for Positive Aging

Ever wondered why a simple sunrise, a mountain view, or even staring at a towering tree makes you feel... small yet profoundly connected? That's *awe*, the emotional cocktail that combines wonder, humility, and a sense of vastness. For older adults, the science of awe offers surprising benefits for mental health, memory, and stress reduction.

What is Awe, Anyway?

Awe is the feeling we get when we're confronted with something vast and beyond our current understanding, often something beautiful or powerful. It's not just poetic—it's a physiological response that can recalibrate our brains. Neuroscience shows that awe activates the parasympathetic nervous system (your "rest and digest" mode) and reduces the body's stress response.

Why Older Adults Need More Awe

As we age, routines can become rigid, and new experiences fewer. This can shrink our cognitive "world." Awe, however, expands it. Research suggests that awe:

1. **Reduces Anxiety:** Awe shifts focus from self to the broader world, reducing self-focused worry.
2. **Boosts Memory:** Novel, awe-inspiring experiences are more likely to stick, improving cognitive retention.
3. **Lowers Stress:** Awe reduces cortisol (the stress hormone), promot- ing relaxation and resilience.
4. **Enhances Social Connection:** Shared awe

moments deepen bonds—think of watching a stunning sunset with a friend.

Nature Walks and Forest Bathing: Awe in Action

Stepping into nature is like opening a portal to everyday awe. Forest bathing (*shinrin-yoku*), the Japanese practice of immersing yourself in a forest environment, enhances this effect. The natural world's grandeur—towering trees, rustling leaves, or the sheer silence—invites awe. Studies show forest exposure lowers blood pressure, heart rate, and stress hormones while boosting mood.

Action Steps:

- **Plan Weekly Nature Walks:** Choose diverse settings—forests, beaches, or gardens—for fresh awe triggers.
- **Create an Awe Journal:** Note one "awe moment" from each outing.
- **Seek Micro-Awe:** Even cityscapes offer wonder. Look up at the night sky or watch clouds drift.

Remember, awe isn't just for mountaintop seekers. It's a daily tool for troubleshooting stress and rediscovering joy—an essential ingredient for thriving at any age.

Reboot Required: Troubleshooting Anxiety, Stress, and

Memory Glitches Or: Why Your Brain Sometimes Feels Like a 1990s Computer (Introducing Memory Castle)

The Memory Castle: A Tour of Your Brain's 5-Star Hotel (My favorite Hack)

Ever forget where you put your keys, or your phone, or that thing you were about to say in the middle of a conversation. It happens to all of us. But what if I told you there's a way to never forget anything again—ever? Welcome to the **Memory Castle**, aka the **Method of Loci**, your very own brain's 5-star hotel for information. Let me give you a quick tour.

A Brief History: The Old-School Memory Hack

The Memory Castle dates all the way back to the **ancient Greeks and Romans**, where it was used by famous orators who needed to remember their speeches. In fact, **Cicero**, the philosopher, was practically the "Google" of his day when it came to remembering things. He didn't just "search" for facts—he had a whole method for locking them away in his mental vault. This vault? The Method of Loci.

The technique was reportedly invented by **Simonides of Ceos** (who sounds like he should be the name of a cool Greek rock band). He apparently used the method after a banquet hall collapsed and, being the memory wizard he

61

was, identified all the victims by remembering where they were sitting. Talk about a memory with *dire consequences*—Simonides was basically the **Sherlock Holmes** of ancient Greece, except instead of magnifying glasses, he used his mind palace.

The Memory Castle: Where Your Thoughts Go to Vacation

Now that you're on board, let me explain the **Memory Castle**—a.k.a. the method that'll help you remember everything from your grocery list to the capital of Bolivia (it's La Paz, by the way). Here's how it works:

1. **Pick Your Palace**: First, you need to pick a place you know like the back of your hand. A house, a childhood treehouse, your favorite park—maybe even your favorite room at your neighbor's house (though it might be awkward when you start walking through their living room mentally storing information). The more familiar the place, the better.

2. **Set Up Your Stations**: Now, take this place and mentally divide it into different rooms, objects, or landmarks. For example, in your home, your kitchen could hold the grocery list, your living room could store your speech, and your bathroom. Well, the bathroom might hold your secrets (or just where you put your car keys).

3. **Visualize the Information**: This is the fun part.

62

Now, place the information you need to remember in these stations. But here's the key: the more bizarre and memorable the image, the better. Imagine walking into your kitchen and seeing a giant watermelon juggling oranges. That's your reminder to buy fruit. Next, head to the bathroom, where a giant toothbrush is holding your speech notes. Yes, it's weird, but that's what makes it stick.

4. **Retrieval Time**: When you need to recall the information, simply take a mental stroll through your castle (I promise it's better than a stroll through the DMV). You'll walk from room to room, retrieving each chunk of information as you go. You'll remember everything, from where you left your phone to where your speech is stored (and you can now give a killer oration on fruit).

Examples of Memory Castle Magic

- **The Grocery List**: Imagine you're walking through your house, picking up strange images. You start in the hallway with a giant loaf of bread sitting on the table. Then you move to the living room, where your couch is covered in eggs (no idea why, but it's memorable). Finally, you enter the bathroom, and, lo and behold, a giant milk carton has tipped over in the sink. When it's time to shop, you'll easily remember your grocery list—no phone or sticky notes required!

- **A Speech**: Picture yourself at a podium in the living room, delivering your speech to an imaginary audience made up of your dog and a few houseplants (they're excellent listeners). Each part of the speech corresponds to a different part of your house—introduction in the foyer, main points in the kitchen, and a grand finale on the porch, where you leave your audience (or dog) in awe. When you need to speak in real life, you can mentally "walk through" your home to remember your speech word-for-word.

- **Remembering Names**: Meet someone new? Store their name in your mind palace. Picture them sitting on your couch with a name tag that says "Samantha." The next time you see her, walk into your living room mentally, and voilà—*you remember her name*, like a pro.

Why the Memory Castle Actually Works (And Doesn't Look Like Hogwarts)

So why does this odd technique work so well? It turns out our brains are hardwired for **spatial memory**. In simpler terms, we're better at remembering things that are physically placed in specific locations. That's why we can remember where we left our keys on the counter, but somehow forget we had keys in the first place. When you pair this spatial advantage with vividly bizarre and emotional images, you've got a powerful recipe for recall.

In short, your Memory Castle isn't just a way to avoid the horror of forgetting your spouse's birthday. It's a fun, quirky mental vacation destination where you can store and retrieve information with ease— like your own personal Hogwarts for the mind. So, next time you need to remember something important, don't just *store* it in your brain—give it a room in your castle! You might even find it more comfortable than your actual living room.

So, use it—or lose it. . .

The brain is a three-pound mass you can hold in your hand that can conceive of a universe a hundred-billion light years across.

-Dr. Marian Diamond

Some years ago, I developed a theory about gender differences and the aging brain, which I will not burden you with here. Confident in the "fact" that I was onto a scientific breakthrough; I decided to contact some leaders in the field of aging and neuroscience.

Top on my list was the distinguished professor of anatomy at U.C. Berkeley, **Dr. Marian C. Diamond**. So, I organized my thoughts in a pithy email and cast it out to the cyber gods like a message in a bottle hoping to reach some distant shore.

The next day I'm going through the usual suspects of email, and I see a reply from Marian Diamond...**THE MARAIAN C. DIAMOND!** My pulse quickened as I fumbled to open this email:

Dear Patrick,

I think you have caught the essence of aging in every sense of the word...the constant flow of new experiences. I don't know if you have come in contact with my Five Basic "Ingredients" for a healthy brain at ANY age. These particular five items were confirmed by experiments in our laboratory.

I. Diet
II. Exercise
III. Challenge
IV. Newness
V. Love

She graciously went on to briefly elaborate on gender differences in the aging brains of rats in her studies. She ended with:

"Just continue to grow your <u>dendrites</u> until well over your 100 years. Warm regards, Marian Diamond."

May years later I still have that email and cherish it...

Dr. Diamond has contributed greatly to our understanding

how the brain works and in turn debunked culturally constructed myths about aging.

Summary and final thoughts

For the unlearned, old age is winter; for the learned it is the season of the harvest.

~ The Talmud

RIPE: Developed to the point of readiness for harvesting (from the author)

As a Boomer, I can honestly say that at this time in my life I am experiencing what it feels like to be "Ripe."

In my love for family and friends, I've never been more deeply moved than I am now.

In my capacity for empathy, I have never been stronger than I am now.

In my work, I've never been more confident in my decision making than I am now.

In my relationships, **I've never been involved in more meaningful connections than I am now.**

In my aesthetic pursuits, I've never been more deeply filled with creativity than I am now.

In my writing, I've never been more deluged with choices of ideas than I am now.

In my decision making, I've never been clearer on what is right for me than I am now.

In my thinking, I've never been a better Idea generator than I am now.

In my moment-to-moment-mindfulness I have never been more present than I am now.

In my understanding of how fortunate I am, I have never been more aware than I am now.

In my health I have never been more caretaking than I am now.

In my life I have never been more aware that my Super-Power lies in choosing what I pay attention to, than I am now.

In my dealing with animals and nature I have never been more conscious than I am now.

In my life I have never been more confident about entering into new adventures and doing things that matter than I am now.

In my life I have never been more open to intuition than I am now. In my life I have never been more comfortable calling out (discerning)

Bullshit, than I am now.

    In my life I've never been more **confident in my contribution**/life's work, than I am now.

In my life I've never been more appreciative of the stewardship I got from the adults in my life, than I am now.

In my life I've never been quicker to reward exceptional behavior than I am now.

In my life I have never been freer to take pure joy in the things I love than I am now.

Can YOU relate?

It feels good to be Ripe.

Robert Browning knew something...

Years may wrinkle the skin, but to give up enthusiasm wrinkles the soul.

~ Samuel Ullman

As the saying goes, ***growing old is not for sissies***, which got me thinking about what they don't tell you about it.

Things They Don't Tell You About Aging

- You will get asked by old friends "Do you still__?" fill in the blank.
- You will reference time in terms of what's left.
- You will most likely become a caregiver for some amount of time (esp. females)
- You will find the closer to death you are the closer to life you are–life's paradox.
- You internalize that nobody gives a f*ck about you or what you're doing.
- You will be the oldest one in the room eventually.
- You will experience your internal world (internality) growing richer.
- You will wear an item of clothing that's 30+ yrs old (hopefully not underwear).
- You will notice exercise becomes a victory over the self.
- You will have boomerang friends that rekindle after the hustle years.
- You will experience The U-shaped Happiness Curve more often.
- You will see your age-related-loss compensation skills skyrocket.

- You will come to embrace slip-on as your new best friend.
- You will capitulate to assistive technology before you are "ready" (e-bike, etc.).
- You will find select friends relative to where you are in life, and much fewer.
- You now think in terms of systems, or whole-picture thinking.
- You find Obituaries interesting, Facebook is how you find out about passing/s.
- You choose comfort over adventure; comfortable adventure is even better.
- You get really savvy at wearing strategic apparel.
- You find experience affords shortcuts.

So don't worry—be happy. . . The best it yet to be.

5

Late Freedom: Don't Give a Sh*t

Freedom—It's a Word That Ignites the Spirit!

~ Unknown

Late Freedom – The Golden Years, Reimagined

Ah, the golden years. The time when you can finally relax, enjoy a little "me time," and—let's be honest—master the fine art of napping without any guilt. But here's the kicker: what if the golden years could be more than just a time to kick back and watch life go by? What if, instead of just marking time, they were the *most* liberated, exciting chapter of your entire life? Enter: **late freedom**—that sweet, paradoxical phase when you're free from, well, *everything*, and free to do *anything*.

What is Late Freedom?

Late freedom is not just about skipping chores (though, let's be real, that's a bonus we all look forward to). Rooted in gerontology—the study of aging—this concept means the moment when you've figured out how to stop playing by other people's rules. You're done with the rat race, you've ditched societal expectations, and now, you get to live life your way. It's when you finally stop worrying about how you *should* live and start doing what makes you feel most like yourself.

Think of it as your personal "I've earned this" phase—not just in terms of relaxation, but in self-expression, too. This is when you can finally give yourself permission to wear mismatched socks, start a new hobby (hello, interpretive dance), or even travel to a country you can't pronounce. The pressure to conform, to fit in, and to check boxes has officially left the building.

The Components of Late Freedom

Freedom from the Tyranny of Time

One of the perks of aging is the ability to set your own schedule—or better yet, forget to set one at all. Remember those days when you lived by the clock? When could a single missed deadline ruin your entire week? Well, forget that. Now, you can enjoy life without the constant TikTok of a schedule pressing on your temples. Want to spend the whole afternoon making perfect pancakes? Go for it. Want to take a two-hour walk to the corner store? Why not! The beauty of late freedom is having time to savor *just being*.

Freedom to Redefine Identity

Did you know that by the time you reach a certain age, you're allowed to say, "You know what? I'm done with the roles that society gave me"? You're free to throw off the shackles of labels like "employee," "parent," or "busy person" and step into something that feels far more authentic. Maybe it's learning how to juggle (literally), becoming the best amateur photographer, or starting your own conspiracy-theory podcast. This is your time to reinvent yourself without the burden of judgment—or, as we like to call it, "the freedom to be gloriously unpredictable."

Freedom from Materialism

Gone are the days of chasing after the latest tech gadget or keeping up with your neighbor's pristine lawn. Late freedom is the sweet release of realizing that stuff isn't what matters most. Instead of spending your weekends browsing malls or accumulating *things*, you find joy in what you *can't* buy: experiences, meaningful conversations, and the serenity that comes from not needing the latest iPhone to feel fulfilled.

Freedom to Make Meaningful Connections

As we age, we become a bit pickier about who we let into our lives. The days of "keeping up appearances" are over.

Late freedom offers the opportunity to focus on the relationships that matter—whether it's a deep connection with an old friend or discovering a kindred spirit at the local book club. Time spent with people who share your values becomes a precious commodity, and the freedom to say "no" to superficial interactions is as satisfying as a five-star dessert.

Freedom to Embrace Mortality

Now, before you panic, we're not saying you should start writing your obituary just yet. But with age comes the realization that, yes, mortality is a thing. And guess what? Accepting it actually sets you free. No longer burdened by the pressure to live up to societal expectations or achieve *something big* by a certain age (you can do it at any age), you can focus on what really matters. And spoiler alert: it's not about being "busy" or "productive." It's about living in the moment, savoring the present, and making peace with the fact that you've already made your mark— whether you realized it or not.

How Late Freedom is Revolutionizing Aging

Gone are the days when "retirement" was synonymous with sitting on the porch in a rocking chair, watching life go by. Thanks to late freedom, older adults are reinventing what it means to age. They're starting second careers, taking up new hobbies, traveling the world, and discovering new passions that they didn't have time for before. Late

Freedom is the antidote to the stereotypical view of aging as a time of decline. It's about vitality, purpose, continued growth and yes, KICKING BUTT!

Why We Should All Be Jealous of Late Freedom

Let's face it, folks: the younger generations could use a little late freedom in their lives. While we're all scrambling to climb the ladder, chasing after promotions and dealing with never-ending to-do lists (stringing beads without a knot on the other end), older generations have cracked the code. They've discovered the secret sauce to a life free from unnecessary stress and unimportant obligations. They've figured out that life isn't about the next promotion or the next shiny object—it's about being present, appreciating the little things, and enjoying the ride. Think of it as Earned Down Time (EDT), and you are fully at choice on how to invest it.

Unselfconsciously Naked

This is an excerpt from Mary Pipher's *Women Rowing North,* a telling narrative of older women's late freedom.

This year I experienced a vivid illustration of the happiness

76

of older women. I switched recreational centers from the university where I have taught for many years to a gym geared toward older people. I noticed a great change in the locker room atmosphere. At the university, the Yong women were mostly stressed and unhappy. They talked on their phones or to their exercise partners about their weight, finances, studies, and relationship issues. Almost all of them hid their bodies by crouching as they undressed. Exempt for occasional happy talk about weekends or school holidays, conversations was generally gloomy.

On the other hand, in my new locker room, we older women walk around unselfconsciously naked or in utilitarian underclothes or swimsuits. Our bodies are saggy with plenty of stretch marks, wrinkles, and cellulite, but do we care? Not much.

We are more interested in each other's faces, which reveal decades of joy and suffering and are often open and awake to the moment.

Older women do talk about their troubles, especially what we call the "organ recitals," that is, conversations about health issues. Mostly, though, we discuss family, travel, books, movies, and fun.

Pipher describes eloquently the everyday experience of "late freedom" for older women in this locker room scenario. She goes on to describe the "almost universal cycle of trauma, despair, struggle, adaptation, and resolution—common to human beings and well known to those of a certain age.

This self-described resilience gained by living over time, Pipher notes, is a wisdom earned by overcoming adversity that hones one's skill in "perspective taking, in managing our emotions, in crafting positive narratives, and in forming intimate relationships."

We Develop the skills of building joy, gratitude, and meaning into every day. By learning these lessons, we cultivate emotional resilience.

~ Mary Pipher, *Women Rowing North*

Late freedom is a byproduct of duration and overcoming adversity— what they used to call good old character building. It's a sweet spot to be in and a powerful one to take advantage of!

To be free of the good opinion of others is liberating, it sometimes takes a while, but you have finally arrived (aka I don't give a SH*T)—Enjoy the ride...

6 Actionable (and Funny) Tips to Exercise Your Late Freedom

1. Embrace the "No-Guilt Nap"

Tip: Set a timer for 30 minutes, grab your comfiest blanket, and proudly announce, "This is a strategic recharge."

Funny Twist: Remember, you're not "napping"—you're conducting an in-depth study on the gravitational pull of your couch.

2. Start a "What the Heck" Hobby

Tip: Always wanted to knit, play the ukulele, or sculpt garden gnomes? Now's the time. Pick something completely random.

Funny Twist: When people ask why you took up competitive whittling, simply say, "Because I can." Bonus points for an intense stare.

3. Declutter Like a Rebel

Tip: Go full Marie Kondo, but with an edge. Keep what sparks joy—and what sparks mischief.

Funny Twist: If you find an old tie-dye shirt from the '70s, put it on and announce, "I'm keeping the spirit alive!"

4. Be Boldly Unapologetic

Tip: Speak your mind, wear a funky hat, or take dance lessons. You've earned it.

Funny Twist: If anyone raises an eyebrow at your choices, reply with, "Sorry, I can't hear you over the sound of my freedom ringing."

5. Reclaim Your Schedule

Tip: Organize your week around pure enjoyment—schedule in hobbies, visits, or that epic TV marathon.

Funny Twist: Rename your calendar events. "Doctor's appointment" becomes "Time-travel health check." Grocery run? "Foraging mission."

6. Practice "Outrageous Generosity"

Tip: Share your time, stories, or quirky skills with others— volunteer or mentor.

Funny Twist: Bring cookies to a neighbor with a note that says, "Made with freedom. Contains no guilt."

Each step lets you lean into life with joy, humor, and a healthy disregard for anyone else's rules. That's Late Freedom in action!

Resources

"Things to Avoid After 75", was the title of an online click-bate article that I didn't take the bait and click on. Instead, what I did do was take the advice of Mark Manson, author of *The Subtle Art of Not Giving a F*ck*—I didn't give it any oxygen. It did move me to make my own list (NOT giving a F*ck of course).

Activities to Avoid After 75

1). Listening to people telling you what to avoid after 75 (that's #1)
2). Ageist attitudes
3). Buying into decline tropes
4). Not calling out ageism when I see it, hear it, or experience it
5). Listening to People telling you when you should retire
6). People who ask, "are you still_____" (fill in the blank)
7). Articles advising what kind of hairstyles/clothes to adopt at this age
8). To go gray or to not go gray? None of your business
9). Lengthy discussions about ailments or competitive complaining
10). Reading media sources saying "Boomers aging in place" are the cause of all the housing ills
11). Being around negative people
12). Wasting time on lost causes
13). Regrets
14). "Age-appropriate" advice
15). SunCity age-segregated communities (unless you choose)

16). "Hot" Investment deals

17). Hoarding

18). Stultifying Routines

19). Heavy Drinking

20). Golf (ok I have a bias)

The message is, online click-bait trolls are noise, static on the line, **ignore and move confidently in the direction of your dreams**—yes, you SHOULD still be dreaming...OK, I violated several of my tenants there, but for a greater point. And besides, I don't give a F*ck...

9 Things I Stopped Giving a Sh*t About After I Turned 50 *by*

Tam Warner Minton

1. What car someone drives or if I've been invited to a party. Just three years ago my husband became critically ill and had a double lung transplant. After that experience, it is hard

to give a shit about the superfluous things in life.

2. Romance.

Seriously? I don't need hearts and flowers and Valentines. My husband is not exactly Mr. Romance, and at this point in my life, I don't want all that crap. As far as sex and intimacy go, I'm old enough to know exactly what I want, so let's just get to it, shall we?

3. Being the perfect parent.

Ha! No one is a perfect parent. No matter what, I am going to screw up. And count on it, my children will remind me of my screw ups much more often than they will talk about all the wonderful things I did for them. I feel good about the way I raised my children, and I have never been burdened with being perfect. Why beat myself up? They turned out well, and I'm proud of the people they have become.

4. Being cool.

I have never been "cool" a day in my life. I'm clumsy, I fall a lot, I'm attention-challenged and can barely keep track of my glasses or my car keys. I'm nerdy about things like English history and taking photos of fish. There is absolutely no point any longer in trying to be cool, so I embrace who I am, and I don't worry about it anymore.

5. Black Friday.

I've never liked shopping that much, but the older I get, the more I shop online. I'd rather join the circus than wait in line at 4 am to go to a store on Black Friday.

6. Pleasing every single person, I care about.

Talk about a way to give yourself a heart attack! I have spent far too much time in my life trying to make other people happy. I have learned that I can't please everybody and not waste time feeling guilty about it. Let people worry about pleasing me for a change.

7. Gossip about movie and tv stars.

Honestly, who are these people? They all look like they are twelve years old. Who gives a shit about what the Kardashians are doing? Robert Kardashian had the bad luck to be pals with OJ Simpson and then die, but why is his family famous for it?

8. Cooking and cleaning.

I have no interest in either, or I cannot get myself motivated to do much in the house, period. I'd rather be with my dogs, kayaking at the lake, writing, looking at my photos, doing yoga, swimming or traveling. In other words, I'd rather do just about anything rather than cook or clean. Nowadays my meals come from My Fit Foods, Simply Fit Meals, or Snap Kitchen. I can barely get motivated to stick my multigrain frozen waffles in the toaster, let alone cook an entire meal.

9. Stuff.

When I hit fifty, I realized that I had a house full of stuff that doesn't really mean much anymore. What am I going to do with all of this stuff? I have to go through it and get rid of it, so I really don't give a shit about getting more, newer, stuff. Have you ever gone to an estate sale and seen all of the stuff people collect in a lifetime and never get rid of? So sad. (source: matadornetwork.com)

Reference

Manson, M. (2016). *The subtle art of not giving a f*ck: A counterintuitive approach to living a good life**. HarperOne.

Pipher, M. (2020). *Women rowing north: Navigating life's currents and flourishing as we age.* Bloomsbury Publishing.

6

Lighten Your Load No One Wants Your Sh*t

Any half-awake materalists well knows—that which you hold holds you.

~ Tom Robbins, 1936

Downsizing can be like hosting a yard sale for emotional baggage—you quickly realize your kids don't want your porcelain penguin collection or those carefully labeled VHS tapes. "It's vintage!" you protest. They reply, "It's clutter." They won't even take Grandma's crocheted doilies. So, why let those treasures gather dust? Sell them! Host a garage sale, go digital on marketplace apps, or barter with neighbors who also thought their kids would treasure their Elvis plate set.

Then, turn that cash into pure fun. Picture this: You sell your old mahogany cabinet, which your kids rejected faster than a fruitcake at Christmas and use the money for a weekend getaway or a tandem skydive. When they ask, "Why didn't you save it for us?" reply, "I did— it funded my skydiving photos. Want one for your wall?" Downsizing isn't letting go; it's upgrading to experiences they'll envy!

Now, let's talk more about downsizing as we age. If you're anything like me, you're either drowning in your own stuff or navigating the clutter left behind by older relatives—let's face it, it's probably both.

George Carlin once famously said, "A house is just a place to keep your stuff while you go out and get more stuff." The man was a prophet. I spent years decluttering the home I grew up in. Years. And by "years," I mean part-time hours squeezed in between, you know, living my life. The house was like a Tetris game where the blocks were made of 60 years of family "treasures," and my parents' motto was clearly "Never throw anything out. You may need it someday."

The space in which we live should be for the person we are becoming now, not for the person we were in the past.

~Marie Kondo, Organizing consultant and Author

Ah, yes, "someday." That's the golden ticket, right? It turns out "someday" is code for "you're inheriting this collection of mystery objects when I'm gone." It's amazing what you find when you finally open the garage: floor-to-ceiling hoarding bliss. And let's not even get into the emotional minefield of "WHO GETS WHAT?" This isn't just spring cleaning—this is an extreme sport. Imagine untangling a lifetime of memories while trying to figure out if Great Aunt Edna's 1983 sweater is a family heirloom or just an itchy thing, you'll end up donating to the nearest thrift store. If you haven't experienced this yet, trust me, you will.

Earlier in life, perhaps it matters less that people cannot park in their garages or close their closet doors. But when hoarding researcher Dr. Ekerdt asked respondents how reluctant they felt about moving, considering the effort required to transfer or dispose of their belongings, he found that 48 percent felt "very reluctant" to move and another 30 percent were "somewhat reluctant." That adds up to more than three- quarters of people over sixty feeling trapped, to some degree, by stuff.

Dante's Inferno

The *Divine Comedy* is a 14th-century epic where Dante, in his dream, sees a beautiful hillside with a paradise at the top, waiting for him to climb. Simple enough, right? But as with all journeys, it's never that easy. Dante gets interrupted by a monster (because of course) who informs him that before he can climb, he must first descend through nine circles of hell, all the way to the bottom, and then climb back up again. As if this wasn't enough of a workout, his guide, the ancient poet Virgil, takes him to the

4th circle, where Dante encounters two warring armies. One shouts, "Why do you hoard?" and the other replies, "Why do you waste?" These poor souls are cursed to push heavy stones, a metaphor for their obsession with wealth and possessions in life, trapping them in hell because they couldn't let go of their stuff.

Fast forward to modern times, and one of my colleagues calls me about an elderly man with a situation very much resembling a *Divine Comedy* of his own—minus the poetic flair. The man, living alone in Portland, Oregon, has turned his home into a fortress of junk. He's not exactly hoarding gold or ancient artifacts, but piles of useless objects— old newspapers, broken furniture, bits of string—have made him a literal prisoner in his own home. This is a textbook case of *Compulsive Hoarding Syndrome* (CHS), which is exactly what it sounds like: a person who can't part with anything, no matter how useless.

The problem is, hoarding isn't just about junk—it's about living spaces so cluttered that they become a health and safety hazard. We're talking beds buried in stuff, kitchens where you can't find the stove (because it's buried under 12 years' worth of expired cans), and fire exits blocked by piles of things that are "too valuable to toss." The challenge? Getting the hoarder to admit there's a problem. It's like asking a fish to admit they're wet. For those who suffer from CHS, getting rid of things isn't just hard—it's a full-blown existential crisis. What's worse, the longer they hang onto these items, the more dangerous it becomes. You're not just dealing with sentimental clutter; you're dealing with living in what could essentially be a fire hazard in the making, surrounded by rats, mold, and the odd collection of expired pet food.

With the aging of the population, hoarding has become one of those "hid- den" challenges that suddenly springs up like a monster in the closet... or, more appropriately, under piles of old newspapers. Compulsive hoarding, which often begins in younger years, really becomes a problem as people age—especially for those with chronic health conditions. As Dr. Randy Frost points out, one of the major issues is mobility; older adults with hoarding tendencies often create "goat-paths" among their clutter, which sounds kind of charming until you realize it's a safety hazard that leads directly to *the floor is lava* territory. Imagine trying to navigate your way through a house that's more like an obstacle course—except instead of cool Ninja Warrior-style challenges, it's just piles of outdated catalogs and ten different types of old plastic containers. Tripping over your own stuff? Oh, that's a *real* risk. And don't even get me started on emergency services trying to reach you when your house is a maze of hoarded treasures. It's less *rescue mission*, more *jungle expedition*.

The irony is hoarders are often perfectionists (sound familiar?) who dread making the wrong decision. They spend so much time "churning" through piles—moving them from one side of the room to the other— that they can't even bring themselves to throw anything out. This indecision is the perfect storm: it's like trying to decide between a million shades of beige, except the stakes are whether or not to toss a 40-year- old toaster. And then there's the emotional side: families often get caught in the crossfire, trying to clean up and organize, only to be met with resistance and guilt.

I personally grew up in a house where visitors were rare—because there was literally nowhere to sit. As for my own journey in de-cluttering my elderly parent's home, it was all-consuming for some time. I was living on the margins of my schedule due to the labor-intensity of dealing with all the stuff. Like most senior care, there are mixed emotions. I want to be there for them–as they were for me. The limited nature of time allocation as a working adult meant there was a big opportunity cost to deal with the vast amount of things accumulated by my parents. Time moving, sorting, selling, donating, recycling, negotiating with siblings (additional stressors here), was precious time away from the people with whom you have limited time left to spend. The lessons here are hard-won—and I pray you do not have the same experience. It will be one of your greatest gifts to leave–a legacy of less for your loved ones. Because in the limited time we have with the people we cherish, it becomes crystal clear that there are no ordinary moments.

Summary

My plea in this chapter is for those who are boomers, GenX and/or older seniors, if you are "over-provisioned" please self-downsize–before it is a crisis and left to loved ones. It will be one of your greatest gifts to leave a legacy of less. I have heard countless times from Millennials they do not want your sh*t!

Working with my mother as she has progressed through four home envi- ronments of decreasing size, I can attest to her comfort at being surrounded by furniture, photos, art, and other objects that are important to her. As she downsizes each time, she feels better that many items that she no longer has room for are going to family members. Now she is down to a tiny fraction of her original household items...and she has found yet another equilibrium in those items.

~ Richard Duncan, Universal Design Institute, Executive Director

I read a disturbing story by **elder law attorney, Geof f Bernhardt** about acouple married for over 50 years. The wife was a compulsive hoarder, and the husband was meticulously clean. The difference was so pronounced they had separate rooms in their home; one jam-packed with stuff, the other meticulously organized. When the wife's health began to decline over time the husband took on the caretaker role. At the end of her life, as she lay dying, her

92

last message to her life-long mate was not **"I love you,"** it was **"please don't touch my stuff."** This heartbreaking story is evidence of a compulsive hoarder.

A big part of getting older and Kicking Butt is lightening up your load. Let's face it: your stuff doesn't spark joy for anyone but you, and maybe not even you anymore. Your kids? They don't want your 47-piece teacup collection or the knickknacks from every road trip since 1972. Millennials are minimalist, eco-conscious, and—let's be real—too broke to store all the "valuable heirlooms" you've stockpiled. And Gen Z? They don't even want houses, let alone the clutter to fill them.

So, here's the deal: start downsizing now, while you're still the one calling the shots. Instead of hoarding "treasures" for some mythical future, trade them in for experiences that you'll remember (unlike the third blender you bought because it was "on sale"). Your legacy isn't in the stuff you leave behind; it's in the laughs, stories, and time you spent with people. Trust me, nobody wants your sh*t—but they *do* want you. So, keep the memories, ditch the mess, and leave a legacy of *less*.

6 Action Steps to Profit from Downsizing

1. Sort and Prioritize

Action: Organize your belongings into categories—keep,

donate, and sell. Prioritize high-value items (furniture, electronics, vintage goods) for resale.

Tip: The "one-year rule" works wonders—if you haven't used it in a year, it's time to say goodbye!

2. Choose the Right Sales Platform

Action: Use the appropriate platforms for different items:

- **Furniture & decor:** Facebook Marketplace, Craigslist
- **Clothing & accessories:** Poshmark, Depop
- **Collectibles & antiques:** eBay, Etsy
- *Tip:* Good photos make a world of difference—bright lighting and clear shots will help you sell quicker!

3. Host a Garage or Estate Sale

Action: Advertise locally (flyers, online posts) and make sure to offer bulk deals for faster sales.

Tip: Offer free coffee and cookies to make your sale a social event—it's more likely to draw in passersby.

4. Utilize Local Resale Shops

Action: Donate or consign your items at local resale shops like Goodwill or Humane Society resale stores. Many of these shops support a cause, making your donation even more rewarding.

Tip: Call ahead to see what they're currently accepting to avoid hauling unwanted items.

5. Bundle Items for Value Deals

Action: Create themed bundles—like kitchen gadgets, books, or vintage decor—where you can price multiple items together for a better deal.

Tip: Buyers love a bonus, so consider throwing in a small, unexpected freebie to make your bundle irresistible!

6. Reinvest the Profits in Experiences

Action: Take your downsizing profits and spend them on an experience—whether that's a mini vacation, a new hobby, or a night out.

Tip: Let your kids know, "Your old toys funded my bucket list!" That's one way to show them how it's done.

Not only will you simplify your space, but you can also help out a good cause by donating to resale shops that support animal welfare, like your local Humane Society resale stores. It's a win-win: declutter, profit, make a difference and Kick Butt!

Success Stories of Decluttering and Kicking Butt

A standout story is of a woman named Christina who

turned her decluttering mission into a thriving online resale business. She started by selling household items, clothes, and furniture through platforms like eBay and Facebook Marketplace. Over time, her knack for identifying valuable items—like vintage glassware or collectibles—helped her transform clutter into a full-fledged income stream. Her biggest lesson? Take high-quality photos, write detailed descriptions, and use local selling apps for bulkier items to save on shipping costs.

Resources: Ways To Turn Your Clutter into Cash [Easy Solutions] Vestlo.com Bosssinglemama.com

Decluttering can not only liberate space but also open surprising

financial opportunities if approached strategically! Let it Go and Kick Butt.

Hoarding

While hoarder personality traits and demographics vary widely, people who live with hoarding disorder often share a set of characteristics.

On average, individuals who exhibit hoarding behavior:

- Live alone
  - Are three times more likely to be obese than the average person

- Are perfectionist
- Have at least one family member who is also a hoarder

Currently, researchers believe compulsive hoarding affects 1 in every 50 people, but it may impact as many as 1 in every 20. According to the National Alliance on Mental Illness (NAMI) Massachusetts, up to 5 percent of the world's population displays symptoms of clinically diagnosable hoarding. (Source: therecoveryvillage.com)

Thanks to R. Frost for The Divine Comedy *story*

Dr. Randy O. Frost is the Harold and Elsa Siipola Israel Professor of Psychology at Smith College and co-author of *Stuff: Compulsive Hoarding and the Meaning of Things* (Houghton, Mifflin, Harcourt, 2010), a book about hoarding for the public. He is an expert on obsessive-compulsive disorder, hoarding, and the pathology of perfectionism, and he has published more than 100 scientific papers on these topics.

His other books on hoarding include *Compulsive Hoarding and Acquiring: Therapist Guide and Workbook* as well as *Buried in Treasures: Help for Compulsive Acquiring, Saving, and Hoarding* (both published by Oxford University Press in 2007). His work on hoarding and its treatment has been funded by the National Institute of Mental Health.

7

Pushing Your Limits as You Age

Push yourself again and again, don't give an inch until the final buzzer.

~ Larry Bird

The Sea Birds: Swimming Against the Tide

One of my favorite websites related to issues of AGING is **boomingen- core.com**. Their content is worth your time and energy because it is relevant to living a fuller life. For example, this morning I read their story **'Pushing Your Limits as You Age,'** it got my attention because this is exactly how I choose to age.

The post includes a brief description then a meaningful and pithy video about a group of mutually supporting women–they call themselves fondly, "The Buckettes" all over the age of 50, who meet, "come rain or shine" for an ocean swim.

As I watched the <u>delightful video</u>, longevity themes easily emerged from the dialogue, secrets to living long and well (and Kicking Butt), surfaced.

LONGEVITY a by-product, not something these women were seeking directly. **No pills, potions, snake oil, gurus, expensive gym member-** ships or expert trainers.

The 10 lessons from the video

Aging is Not a Limitation, It's a New Chapter

- **Lesson:** Aging isn't something to fear or resist—it's an opportunity for growth, exploration, and discovery. Just because you've grown older doesn't mean you're incapable of doing new things, having fun, or embracing life with vigor.
- **Application:** The Sea Birds show that age is not a barrier to adventure or self-improvement. Whether it's trying new activities or finding new purpose, aging can open doors to new experiences.

The Power of Consistency

- **Lesson:** Consistency in healthy habits, like swimming, can have profound benefits for both physical and mental well-being. Regular engagement in an activity, even something as simple as a morning swim, builds strength, resilience, and camaraderie.
- **Application:** Regular commitment to an activity can

100

help maintain both physical health and mental clarity, regardless of age. Consistency builds confidence, connection, and long-term benefits.

Community and Connection Are Vital

- **Lesson:** The importance of community cannot be overstated. The Sea Birds demonstrate how shared experiences—whether it's swimming in the ocean, facing challenges, or celebrating victories— create deep bonds and provide support, especially as we age ("social capital").
- **Application:** Building strong, supportive relationships in later life **is key to well-being. Whether it's friends, family, or groups like the Sea Birds, connection helps people feel less isolated and more empowered.**

Embrace the Unpredictability of Life

- **Lesson:** The ocean represents the unpredictability of life. Just like the waves, life can be rough and challenging, but it is also full of beauty and opportunity. The Sea Birds embrace the challenges, showing that life's unpredictability doesn't need to be feared but navigated with courage.
- **Application:** Life after a certain age doesn't need to be rigid or predetermined. Instead of fearing the unknown, embrace it with curiosity and openness.

Be ready to adapt, swim through, and enjoy what comes.

Facing Fears Brings Freedom

- **Lesson:** The Sea Birds face the cold, the uncertainty, and even their own insecurities by jumping into the ocean each day. The water is a metaphor for life's challenges, and facing those challenges head-on with others can be freeing.
- **Application:** By confronting fears—whether physical, emotional, or social—people often find a sense of freedom and empowerment. Taking that first step into the unknown leads to growth and strength.

Physical Activity Can Rejuvenate the Spirit

- **Lesson:** Staying physically active, particularly in nature, has rejuvenating effects on both the body and mind. Swimming in the ocean not only strengthens the body but also nourishes the spirit.
  - **Application:** Regular physical activity, especially in natural settings, can be a form of self-care that revitalizes your energy, boosts mood, and improves overall well-being.

102

Aging Well Within One's Age Means Accepting Change

- **Lesson:** Aging doesn't mean stopping—it means accepting change and embracing the different stages of life. The Sea Birds' ability to find peace with the natural changes of their bodies and lives is a powerful reminder of how to age gracefully.
- **Application:** Embracing change is essential to aging well. Accepting the changes in the body and mind without regret or resistance is a key to mental and emotional peace in later years.

Friendship and Humor Are Essential to Longevity

- **Lesson:** The Sea Birds laugh together, share stories, and support one another. Their bond helps them to not only face the physical demands of swimming but also the emotional challenges that come with aging. Humor and lightness keep the group grounded and joyful.
- **Application:** Maintaining a sense of humor and strong friendships is vital for emotional health. Finding joy in life, even with the challenges, helps sustain resilience and happiness.

Legacy is About More Than Years Lived

- **Lesson:** Legacy is created by the lives we touch and the experiences we share. The Sea Birds' story isn't just about their time in the ocean; it's about the lessons they teach and the impact they have on others. They create a ripple effect in their community.

- **Application:** Leave a legacy by making an impact on others— whether through mentorship, shared experiences, or simply showing others how to live well at any age. Legacy isn't just about the number of years but about the quality of those years and the connections made.

Nature Has Healing Power

- **Lesson:** The ocean offers more than just physical benefits. It's a source of emotional healing, providing clarity, peace, and strength. The natural world can be a refuge for those seeking restoration and grounding.
- **Application:** Spending time in nature, whether by the ocean, in the mountains, or in a local park, can provide the mental and emotional space needed for healing and reflection.

These lessons underscore the themes of empowerment, resilience, and community that permeate the story of the Sea Birds. They remind us that aging is not something to fear but something to embrace fully with strength, support, and a sense of adventure.

104

The Story of the Sea Birds "The Buckettes"

The sun was just beginning to rise over the horizon, casting a golden glow on the ocean. The early morning mist hung in the air like a soft whisper, and the sea stretched out before them, endless and inviting. For the women who had gathered at the beach that morning, the ocean was more than just a body of water—it was their sanctuary, their challenge, their friend. They were the Sea Birds, a group of older women who had discovered something extraordinary: the power of the ocean to heal, empower, and connect.

Margaret was the first to arrive, as she always was. At 68, she had a presence about her—tall, lean, and somehow always looking as if she were on the cusp of something exciting. She stood with her toes in the sand, watching the waves break rhythmically against the shore. The air was cool, the water even colder, but it didn't matter. To Margaret, there was nothing quite like the feeling of plunging into the ocean, feeling the cold bite of the water against her skin, and letting the waves wash away the weight of the world.

When Margaret had first moved to the coastal town, she hadn't expected to find anything like the Sea Birds. She was retired now, having spent years as a high school teacher, and though she'd loved the idea of living by the sea, something was missing. She wasn't ready to just sit on her porch and watch the waves. She wanted more. So, one morning, on a whim, she put up a flyer at the local community center.

"Looking for a few brave souls to join me for early morning swims in the ocean. No experience necessary, just a love for the sea and a willingness to dive in. Meet me at 6 AM by the rocks."

She didn't expect much. But the next morning, when she showed up, there were two women waiting for her. Anne, who was full of energy despite being well into her seventies, and Dolores, a quiet woman who had recently retired from a career in finance. The three of them hesitated for a moment, feeling the cold air, staring at the wild surf. Then, without another word, they walked into the waves, slowly at first, the cold water shocking their skin.

They swam together in silence, but it wasn't awkward—it was peaceful. The rhythmic sound of the water, the coolness of the sea, the way their bodies felt alive in the water—it was all the motivation they needed. From that day forward, they met every morning, sometimes with just the three of them, sometimes with more. The Sea Birds, as they came to call themselves, were born.

As the weeks went on, the group grew. Lila, a former nurse with a sharp sense of humor, joined after hearing about it from a neighbor. Linda, who had once been a competitive swimmer in her youth but hadn't set foot in a pool in decades, showed up one morning with a nervous smile. June, a grandmother who had recently moved to the town to be closer to her family, came along after her daughter gently encouraged her to get out of the house.

Each of them had their own reasons for showing up at the beach that morning. For some, it was a way to stay active. For others, it was a way to feel connected to something greater than themselves. For all of them, it became a lifeline. The ocean was their place of refuge, a place to shed the weight of the world and simply be. And through those early morning swims, they came to understand something deeper: they weren't just swimming against the tide of the ocean—they were swimming against the tide of time, refusing to let aging dictate the way they lived.

The Sea Birds learned quickly that the ocean was not always kind. The water could be rough, the currents unpredictable, and the temperature— especially in the winter—frigid. But it was precisely this harshness that gave them strength. Every morning, they arrived at the beach with the same purpose: to face the ocean, to dive in, and to find peace in the chaos. The cold didn't deter them. Instead, it became a challenge—a way to prove to themselves that they could still do something bold, something brave. And they did it together.

There were moments when the waves were too strong,

when the sea seemed to fight back, and they had to turn back, breathless and laughing. There were days when they stood on the shore, hesitant, unsure of whether they could push through. But more often than not, the Sea Birds found their rhythm. They found a way to move together, to glide through the water with a grace that belied their years.

In the water, they didn't think about their ages. They didn't think about their wrinkles or their aches or their fears about growing older. They didn't think about the aches in their bones or the memory lapses that seemed to come with age. They just swam. The ocean didn't care how old they were. It didn't care if they had wrinkles or gray hair or if they moved slower than they once did. The ocean only cared if they were willing to dive in and face it head-on.

There was something magical about the way the ocean soothed them, too. The salt water had a way of healing— not just their bodies, but their hearts. It was as if the ocean could take all their grief, their worries, their regrets, and wash them away. Dolores, who had lost her husband several years ago, found solace in the waves. Anne, whose children had long since moved away, found a sense of peace she had never expected. Margaret, who had spent years pouring her energy into her students, found that the ocean was the only place where she could truly unwind. And Lila—always the life of the group—found that the ocean could give her the kind of clarity that no doctor's appointment ever could.

They weren't just swimming; they were healing, together. And in that healing, they found strength.

But it wasn't just the ocean that bonded them. It was each other. The Sea Birds became a support system in ways none of them had anticipated. They began to share more than just the ocean. They shared stories of their lives, their struggles, their joys. They talked about their families, their fears, their dreams. And through their swims, they realized that aging didn't mean retreating—it meant embracing life in all its complexity, its beauty, and its messiness.

As the seasons passed, the Sea Birds became more than just a group of women swimming together. They became a symbol—of resilience, of friendship, of what it means to age with grace and power. They no longer worried about what the world thought of them. They knew they were strong. They knew they were capable. And as they swam together, they knew they were part of something bigger than themselves.

They weren't just swimming against the tide of the ocean. They were swimming against the tide of time itself.

And in doing so, they had found a new kind of freedom.

The Sea Birds had come to understand that age wasn't a barrier. It was an opportunity to dive deeper, to embrace the waves, and to live life as fully as the ocean allowed— and of course Kick Butt!

(Source: Amanda Woods)

Do you hear The Call?

Throughout your life, there is a voice only you can hear. A voice which mythologists label "The Call." A call to the value of your own life. The choice of risk and individual bliss over the known and secure. You may choose not to hear your spirit. You may prefer to build a life within the compound, to avoid risk. It is possible to find happiness within a familiar box, a life of comfort and control. Or, you may choose to be open to new experiences, to leave the limits of your conditioning, to hear the call.

Then you must act. If you never hear it, perhaps nothing is lost. If you hear it and ignore it, your life is lost.

–Jennifer James, PhD

Windows: Success is the Quality of Your Journey (1987)

The Call

This idea of a mythological call is a personal favorite of mine and a reoccurring theme in my own life—and I will

110

bet in yours too. Stephen Covey once said "what's most personal is most universal. In the past when I did a "life review" and saw turning points when something was compelling me to take a leap of faith, I could only define it as a restless feeling. I really had no language for that *"something"* until I heard Jean Houston describe The Hero's Journey. Mythologist, Joseph Campbell described The Hero's Journey in his book; *The Hero With a Thousand Faces (1949).* Campbell found that many cultures have a sequential pattern to their myth making—that is, the same steps play out in stories from different cultures.

The steps of the Hero's Journey:

1) Innocence (comfortable with your situation)
2) The Call to Adventure (now aware of your challenge)
3) Initiation (you are being tested)
4) Allies (finding help)
5) Breakthrough (getting new awareness or resolution)
6) Celebration (return home, changed)

George Lucas read *The Hero With a Thousand Faces* and it was inspired by Star Wars—in fact many movies use this same template over-and-over (See any Kevin Costner movie). The Call is really about a passage, advancing from one stage to another. This concept has been written about by many thinkers, but none more eloquently than H.R. Moody in *The Five Stage of The Soul (1997).* Dr. Moody is one of the most innovative thinkers on gerontology alive

111

today. His unique treatment of The Call (and subsequent stages) has a spiritual basis. He states: "Sometimes The Call reveals itself in dreams."

The Dream (Author's note)

In 2007 I was in contact with H.R. Moody concerning a major passage in my life. One night I had a dream I was standing in a batter's box awaiting my turn at bat. A young batgirl in a brightly flowered dress was mocking me as she handed me my bat. I gazed towards home plate and standing there was young Ted Williams in his prime. His cotton uniform was cinched tightly around his trim waist with a belt and his hair was glossy black. He turned to look over his left shoulder at me standing in the circle—then winked and said:" You're next kid." In the dream I glanced down at my right foot wearing baseball cleats as it broke the plane of the chalk line of the on-deck circle.

I seldom remember dreams, but this one was too meaningful. Moody, an expert in dream analysis, describes the Judas inside all of us as; "a heedless, worldly naysayer who looks for the slightest opportunity to abort our journey and betray our highest yearnings" (p. 150). In the dream, as I see it, the batgirl represented my Judas—the naysayer in me. The good news is I left the safety of the on-deck circle (the passage) and headed for home plate to take my turn at bat. It was just as Dr. Moody suggested, The Call to a larger self was revealed in a dream with a baseball metaphor.

Aging is a passage for all of us fortunate to live long enough to create history. When we look back on turning points we can determine how, and if, The Call was answered. When we look to the future, we may have more awareness to identify those feelings of being constructively discontent as, *The Call.* Insights provided by scholars like H.R. Moody give us language for our experiences and like a rock climber; we have a toehold (terms and concepts) from which to climb higher to a greater understanding.

Conquering any difficulty always gives one a SECRET JOY, for it means pushing back a boundary line and adding to one's liberty.

-Henri Frederic Ameil

Self-Efficacy

Psychologist Dr. Albert Bandura developed a theory that is useful not only in the field of psychology but gerontology (aging) as well. The concept is called "Self-efficacy," and it can serve you well when you know about it.

A WEAK self-efficacy includes the following:

~Avoid challenges

~Believe difficult tasks and situations are beyond your capabilities

~Focus on personal failings and negative outcomes

~Quickly lose confidence in personal abilities

A STRONG self-efficacy on the other hand includes:

~View challenges and problems as tasks to be mastered

~Develop deeper interests in activities in which you participate

~You form a stronger sense of commitment to your interests and activities

~You recover quicker from setbacks and disappointments

Can you see how having a STRONG self-efficacy might play a role in your growing older and Kicking Butt!

Here is the clinical version (dry academic but to the point)

Self-efficacy, a core concept in Albert Bandura's social cognitive theory, is influenced by four primary sources: mastery experiences, vicarious experiences, verbal persuasion, and emotional and physio- logical states. **Mastery experiences** are the most powerful source, as successfully completing tasks reinforces confidence in one's abilities and provides a foundation for tackling future challenges. **Vicarious experiences** involve observing others perform tasks successfully, which can instill a belief that similar outcomes are achievable. This is particularly impactful when the observer identifies with the person they are watching. **Verbal persuasion** refers to encouragement or positive reinforcement from others, which can strengthen an individual's belief in their capacity to succeed, especially when the feedback comes from a trusted source. Lastly, **emotional and physiological states**—such as stress, anxiety, or physical fatigue—can affect self-efficacy. Managing these states effectively can enhance confidence, as a calm, composed mindset is often conducive to better performance. Together, these four sources shape our perception of capability and influence our ability to confront and overcome challenges.

Here is the translation (in plain English):

*Self-efficacy: a fancy term for believing you can handle life's curveballs without tripping over your own feet. It's powered by four main sources, kind of like a superhero's toolkit. First up: **mastery experiences**—the gold standard. Imagine finally assembling that IKEA bookshelf without leftover screws. Nailed it! Every success boosts your confidence. Then there's **vicarious experiences**, or the "if they can do it, I can too" effect. Watching someone else conquer a challenge makes you think, "Hey, I've got* this!"—*especially if they're your age or skill level. Next, we've got* **verbal persuasion**: *those pep talks from friends, family, or your overly enthusiastic barista. A well- timed "You've got this!" can work wonders, especially when it's not followed by "...right?" Finally, there's* **emotional and physiological states**. *Feeling calm and collected? You're ready to take on the world. Nervous, jittery, or in desperate need of a bathroom? Maybe not so much. Keep these four tools sharp, and you'll feel like the self-efficacy superhero you were always meant to be.*

Theme: Turning Points (late-in-life transcendence / Self-Efficacy in Practice)

I have always been drawn to stories of personal transformation, or "turning points" in people's lives. The appeal for me is in the notion of change—your foreseeable life suddenly takes a new turn.

I had just such a moment in 1997 when an injury caused great loss leading to a re-evaluation in my life as the scaffolding (metaphor) crumbled around me. I had always been the athlete; and that was now threatened. Not having my body readily available to me caused me to consider physical frailty for the first time. I then learned; **your challenges will come from what you most lean on in life.** I had leaned on my physicality, and for a painful period, it was taken from me.

116

Someone awfully close to me shared a story of a turning point in her life the night she realized she was mortal and going to someday die. She laid in a fetal position on the floor of her kitchen weeping uncontrollably— alone; what the medieval mystics called "the dark night of the soul." It was a reality confronting experience that made her stronger in the long run.

Normative Transitions vs. Turning Points

As human beings we all experience turning points in our lives. Several longitudinal studies have documented that most Americans report (often several) turning points.

Clasen studied 268 subjects in their mid-fifties or early sixties and found that "more than 85% did feel that there had been turning points in their lives, and most could identify more than one." For men and women, marriage and career events were most frequently mentioned as turning points; and were associated with greater personal autonomy, a different self-concept, and more confidence.

These kinds of normative transformations like leaving home and/or choosing a vocation, are on-course and "appropriate" for the chrono- logical age. But what interests me most are the turning points which are **discontinuous** and late-life, with what would be predicted from past life experience and move the individual in a different direction.

According to Harven and Masoaka, normative transitions become turning points when; 1) they coincide with or are followed by a crisis; 2) are accompanied by family conflict; 3) lead to unexpected consequences; or 5) require constant adjustments.

Late-in-Life Discontinuous Changes

For years I have kept an article (since 1994) titled; ***"The Unflinching Eye of Elizabeth Layton."*** It is a tale of a late bloomer, the creative spirit, and **the transformative power of turning points.**

Layton lived some 30 years tormented with the perils of depression in Wellsville, Kansas. This woman had undergone shock treatments, tried medications, and psychotherapy—all failed to bring her spirit alive. The death of a child in 1976 plunged her further into the darkness and at the age of 68 she felt at the end of her rope.

The turning point came when her sister suggested she enroll in a drawing class at the local university; there she learned contour drawing (the artist draws while looking at the object, never taking her eye off the subject matter, or lifting the pencil off the paper).

One evening her husband was out, so she decided to follow through on her assignment of a self-portrait. Peering into a small mirror she began to draw the contours of her face—at 68 it was not what she wanted to see. She had wrinkles, flabby skin, age spots, arthritic fingers, and a body too large...but she drew what she saw.

The drawings were unlike anything her teacher, friends, or family had ever seen. Drawing obsessively for 10 hours a day for the next 6 months, she realized at the end of that period **the depression as gone.**

Her drawings won worldwide acclaim and have been exhibited across the country including the Metropolitan Museum of Art in New York City and The National Museum of American Art in Washington, D.C., as well as featured in *People, Life,* and *Parade* magazines.

Laytons' work takes head-on the social issues of the time—the homeless, capital punishment, racial prejudice, and women's rights. And she is best known for her portrayals of old age.

Two works which exemplify her subject matter are *"The Motherless Child"* which is a series of 16 drawings, was inspired by weekly visits to her 91-year-old aunt in a nursing home; and *"My Own Gulliver in Lilliput"* showing Mrs. Layton tied to the ground, hamstrung by childishness, jealousy, timidity, laziness, and fear of mother's disapproval—emotions that cause havoc in women's lives.

Mrs. Layton died in 1993 at the age of 83, but not before discovering that it is never too late to become what you might have been.

The take home message for this chapter is getting older and Kicking Butt calls for a strong Self-Efficacy and pushing your limits. Now, try it at the deep end. . .

Resource

See Elizabeth Layton.com The Video The Sea Birds

Pushing Your Limits As You Age: When was the last time you pushed yourself? Here's a wonderful story of how some women are doing this and building friendships in the process. Found: https://boomingencore.com/pushing-your-limits-as-you-age-aac778af-d2ac-4b60-8db0-698118466d27

> *When we got out there I asked how deep it was – I'd never been anywhere I couldn't touch the bottom. And when they said, 'It's quite deep,' I swung around and squealed with delight to think that I was in deep water.*

Source: Mina learnt to swim at 62 – now she's in the ocean every day *By* Amanda Woods / *https://www.smh.com.au/lifestyle/life-and-relationships/mina-learnt-to-swim-at-62-now-she-s-in-the-ocean-every-day-20220126-p59req.html*

120

Reference

Hareven, T. K., & Masaoka, K. (1988). Turning Points and Transitions: Perceptions of the Life Course. *Journal of Family History*, *13*(1), 271-289. James, J. (1987). *Windows: Success is the quality of your journey.* Addison- Wesley.

Moody, H. R., & Carroll, D. (1997). *The five stages of the soul: Charting the spiritual passages that shape our lives.* Doubleday.

Starr JM. Peace Corps service as a turning point. Int J Aging Hum Dev. 1994;39(2):137-61. doi: 10.2190/1206-9618-DFJ2-M6TX. PMID: 8002098.

8

Myth: Successful Aging is Ageless Aging

A Chinese proverb says that we naturally see the beauty of youth but must learn to see the beauty of age.

Ageless Aging is a Myth

Since January 1, 2011, the demographic transition became real for baby boomers, the oldest turned 65. This often-stated fact is becoming hackneyed now, but the reality is still settling in for many; however uneasy it makes us all feel. For the next decade, 10,000 baby boomers a day will reach this milestone. Which has led to an exuberance with which our culture has (mainly boomers born 1946-1964).

Newsweek contributing author Susan Jacoby notes, the fact is as we age, physical and financial hardships mount as people move beyond the relatively hardy 60s and 70s ("young-old") and the territory gets harsher into 80s and 90s (old-old). The incidence of Alzheimer's disease is 50% for those over the age of 85; and two-thirds of Americans older than 85 are women, who usually become poorer with age. The message is defying age comes at a cost. Further,

123

Jacoby reports that age-defying hope and hype do nothing to address the over-whelming political issue of how to pay for Medicare and Social Security, or the many personal decisions about aging in place, retirement, or end-of-life issues that are just offshore brewing. Jacoby also warns that many of us must prepare for the possibility that not the best, but some of the worst years of our lives may lie ahead if we live to the oldest-old age group.

Oh, there's plenty of advice out there on aging—some solid, some straight-up snake oil. You know the type: "Drink this magic tea, and you'll reverse time like Benjamin Button!" But one definition stands out in its absurdity: *Successful Aging means maintaining all the abilities you had at 25.* Right. Because who doesn't want to run marathons, chug tequila, and pull all-nighters in their 70s? (Actually, some people still try... *Respect.*)

This definition clings to youth like a koala on an espresso binge, refusing to acknowledge that—surprise! —we change. If you stubbornly hang on to the values of youth, obsessing over gym selfies, six-packs, and corporate conquests well into your golden years, you might be on a one-way ticket to a midlife crisis sequel.

A better approach? Embrace the YOUR evolution of aging. Instead of fixating on what you've lost—like hair or the ability to recover from hangovers—celebrate what you've gained. Wisdom, perspective, and the kind of confidence that only comes from knowing you can wear socks with sandals and *not care*.

Age isn't just "the absence of youth." It's the Third Act, baby! And in this act, you're the star.

Betty Friedan noted:

"An accurate, realistic, active identification with one's own aging – as opposed both to resignation to the stereotype of being 'old' and denial of age changes," according to Freidan, "seems an important key to vital aging and even longevity."

Betty nailed it (decades ago), a sweet spot—she once said that we must live our own age. When (and if) you ask yourself: "What's my future going to look like?" And in your mind's eye, it looks like it does now, you are at risk for Hyper-habituation, stagnation, and development may be sacrificed at the altar of the illusion of stability. Friedan noted, *"The old Americans I studied do not perceive meaning in aging itself; rather, they perceive meaning in being themselves in old age" (1986, p. 6)*.

Geriatrician Muriel R. Gillick, in her book "The Denial of Aging," emphasizes the social consequences of faith in an ageless old age: "If we assume that Alzheimer's disease will be cured and disability abolished in the near term," she writes, "we will have no incentive to develop long- term-care facilities that focus on enabling residents to lead satisfying lives despite their disabilities." More important, blind faith in medical solutions prevents discussion about the urgent non-medical needs of the old. Americans need not only better long-term-care facilities for the sickest old but community-based services to foster independence for the healthier old. The article ends by stating that only when we abandon the fantasy that age can be defied, will we begin a conversation based on reason and not on yearning for a fountain of youth, and figure out how to make 90 a better 90—AMEN!

Falsehood is invariably the child of fear in one form or another.

~ Aleister Crowley

The messaging here may seem dis-spiriting, especially to women who are long-lived, but I assure you it can be just the opposite. It is a wake-up call to viewing aging not solely as the absence of youth, but instead as a call to live fully within each age and make the future a part of your current philosophy. What is needed is a more empowering approach to your future-self, because the future of aging belongs mainly to women—the demographic trend is towards a feminized gerontocracy (older women rule the world).

According to the 2018 Profile of Older Americans, in 2017,

among the population age 65 and over there were 28.3 million women and 22.6 million men, or a sex ratio of 125 women for every 100 men. At age 85 and over, this ratio increased to 184 women for every 100 men. And as of this writing (November 2024), the oldest person living is Tomiko Itooka (Japan, b. 23 May 1908), who is 116 years and 116 days old, as verified in Ashiya, Hyogo, Japan, on 16 September 2024. The oldest verified person to ever live was a French woman, Jeanne Calment, who died at 122 years, 164 days in 1997.

Women still outlive men by about 5 to 6 years and the theories range from biological, behavioral, and sociological, and have been bandied about in pool halls and academic halls alike—most likely it is a hybrid of each (and some unknown X factor). But the fact remains, men do get old—but women get older. There is a recreating afoot of what growing older as a woman has in store for you.

(Author Side note: Tell the men you know that if they keep their shelf-life up their dance card will always be filled!)

Aging is Trending

The trend is clear: we're living longer than we did, and it doesn't look like that's going to change anytime soon. In fact, it seems the future is all about *maturity*—specifically, female maturity. At the turn of the 20th century, life expectancy at birth was only 46 years for men and 48 years for women. By midcentury, life expectancy was around 66 years for men and 71 years for women. In the most recent years, life expectancy has increased to 76 years for men and 81 years for women. so now it's time to rewrite how we view those golden years. Instead of clinging to the past like a vintage leather jacket, why not find a balance between who you were, who you are, and who you're becoming? Think of it as a personal makeover that doesn't involve any questionable Botox decisions. You've got a whole lifetime of experience under your belt; now let that mature wisdom guide you into a rewarding next chapter.

The way we think about aging has been evolving for some time, but if you open a book on old age, the first thing you'll probably see is a slew of panic-inducing statistics about how fast, how soon, and how *much* the elderly population will grow. It's like they're trying to convince us that retirement home bingo is just around the corner for everyone. These doom-and-gloom predictions are a relic of historical gerontology—the science of aging that used to be obsessed with pathology, decline, and, frankly, making old age sound like one big medical emergency. Before that, aging was just a mysterious existential problem, like a riddle no one wanted to solve. But with the rise of modern medicine, aging got a serious makeover from a mysterious life phase to a biomedical issue.

In the past 100 years, the average lifespan has increased by about 25 years. At the same time, we've increased the burden of disease. We're living longer, but not healthier. Most chronic diseases and cancers occur in the later part of life, in the 25 years of life we've gained thanks to modern medicine. Is that a good trade off?

~ Elizabeth Huges MD

Now, don't get me wrong—disease and disability that come with aging are very real, (no happy gerontology here) but the idea that we're doomed to an inevitable decline is starting to feel a bit outdated. More people are realizing that we *can* extend vitality well into advanced years—*if* we embrace the possibility of growth rather than just default to decay.

So, given Dr Huges's question, I'm sharing a personal story of meeting someone who changed my view of what's possible in old age. In part because she was an example of getting older and Kicking Butt!

Mavis Lindgren: Grandma Wears Running Shoes

A critical care nurse, Patrick Roden, was a medical volunteer at the Portland Marathon of 1992 when he came to the aid of the celebrated 85-year-old marathoner, Mavis Lindgren. They became fast friends, and he was her escort for many marathons until her last at age 90. "Mavis changed the way I viewed aging," Patrick said, "The

129

medical model tends to focus on what goes wrong in aging–and neglects to inform us about what goes right. She inspired me to begin working on a Ph.D. in aging and human development."

My Story

Night's chill lingered in the air and the silence was broken by the sounds of songbirds. The sun was just beginning to rise on a crisp October morning in 1992. Suddenly the squeaking brakes of a rental truck and the clanging of folding chairs shattered the serenity. With military precision, the volunteers began to set up the first aid station at the 18-mile marker. I was one of those volunteers and this was the annual running of the Portland Marathon.

It took an hour to set up and go through my checklist. The first aid kit was in order and the communications were working. We were ready. Soon the elite runners would be flying through, followed by a seemingly endless sea of participants. The conditions were perfect: a bright clear indigo sky, golden fall leaves. All of us were anticipating an inspiring day.

The morning had been uneventful at our station. The usual blisters, Vaseline applied to the chaffed skin, hydration to the dehydrated, and lots of moral support. One pregnant woman reached the 18-mile point and could go no further so we loaded her into the ambulance. They taxied her to the finish line and her anxiously awaiting husband.

It was now late afternoon, and the sea of runners had dwindled to a trickle of determined souls. The frequent and now familiar static that preceded a message from the EMS broke the airwaves. An elderly woman was reported down near the 18-mile mark, in our territory. I waited for a person fitting the description to pass, and no one did. Strapping on my first aid kit, I set out to investigate.

Running upstream, I began to think, how elderly could they mean? Whoever it was, he or she had gone 18 miles, and this was a marathon after all...50, maybe 60, I thought.

As I rounded the bend, I saw a young woman attending the injured runner who looked like Mother Theresa in running shorts! The young woman explained that another runner had cut in front of the injured woman and knocked her down as she stepped towards the curb. As I listened, I assessed the situation. The injuries included an obviously fractured wrist as well as a small bump on the head. "Her name is Mavis," the young woman said.

"Mavis, I would like to escort you to the first aid station," I began... "Young man, I'm going to finish this race," she politely interrupted. After a few seconds of negotiating, I held up her injured arm and we briskly took off for the station (or so I thought).

Amazed, I blurted out "How old are you?" "I'm 85." She pointed to her number pinned to the front of her T-shirt. "Every year, they give me the number of my age. This year I'm number 85. "What do you mean each year?" I asked.

Mavis Lindgren had run all over the world. She had appeared many times on TV, radio, and magazines such as Runner's World, Sports Illustrated, and The New York Times, and been mentioned in books such as Age Wave (Ken Dychtwald) and Grandma Wears Running Shoes (Patricia Horning Benton). She was no stranger to Portland, either. All along the course, there were signs encouraging her and the cheers followed her every step! Two middle-aged women ran up and hugged her exclaiming that they wanted to be just like her when they grew up.

Mavis and I reached the finish line arm-in-arm, right into interviews for the 6'oclock news (I have the video). I was asked to escort her to the entire race the next year in 1993, and it became a tradition.

She retired from running at age 90 after the 1997 marathon. It was her 75th and final 26.2-mile outing. Phil Knight of Nike had a custom pair of "Air Mavis" running shoes made especially for her final marathon. Her two daughters and grandchildren accompanied us and it was an emotional finale to an illustrious running career.

What makes her story all the more exceptional to me is that at age 62, Mavis was leading a sedentary life, spending most of the time reading, writing, and knitting. She had suffered four bouts of pneumonia in five years and, as a retired nurse, she knew the antibiotics weren't the long-term solution. Something had to change. A doctor urged her to join an early birds walking group. At age 70, encouraged by her son, she ran her first marathon! Two years later, she established a record of 4:33.05, and for the next eight years, held world's best time for women 70 and over. And at 84 she finished the Los Angeles marathon in 6 hours 45 minutes-the fastest woman in her age category. "After I started running, I never had another cold," she said.

Asked what his message was, Gandhi replied: **"My life is my message.** "This could well be said about Mavis Lindgren. Mavis never was about "ageless aging," in fact she often touted "I'm having fun being an old lady!"

It was formerly a terrifying view to me that I should one day be an old woman. I now find that Nature has provided pleasure for every state.

~Mary Worley Montagu

"Ageless aging" suggests the possibility of aging without experiencing some of the typical physical and cognitive declines associated with getting older. It implies

133

maintaining youthful characteristics, health, and vitality despite advancing in years. The term is often used in marketing and wellness contexts to promote books, products, services, or lifestyles that claim to help people not age (anti-aging) and maintain a youthful appearance and functionality forever. It's pretty to think so (thanks Ernest Hemingway), but it can be psychologically damaging to think getting old happens to everyone else. News flash, it even happened to Dick Clark (eventually).

Key Aspects of "Ageless Aging"

Youthful Appearance:

- Emphasis on maintaining a youthful look through skincare, cos- metic procedures, and other aesthetic treatments.

Health and Vitality:

- Focus on sustaining physical health, energy levels, and overall well- being through diet, exercise, and possibly supplements.

Cognitive Function:

- Strategies to preserve or enhance cognitive abilities and mental sharpness as one ages.

Lifestyle Choices:

- Promotion of lifestyle habits that purportedly contribute to a more youthful and healthy aging process, such as stress management, sleep quality, and social engagement.

Misleading Aspects

Unrealistic Expectations:

- It can create unrealistic expectations about the aging process, as it suggests that one can completely avoid the natural signs and effects of aging.

Contradictory Concept:

- The term itself is contradictory because aging inherently involves changes and declines in certain physical and cognitive functions.

Commercial Exploitation:

- Often used as a marketing gimmick to sell products and services with claims that may not be scientifically supported.

Neglect of Natural Aging Process:

- By focusing on "agelessness," it might downplay the importance of accepting and adapting to the natural aging process.

Conclusion:

While "ageless aging" promotes a positive outlook on maintaining health and vitality, it's important to approach it with a realistic understanding of what can be achieved. The concept can be motivating for adopting healthier lifestyle choices but should not overshadow the natural and inevitable aspects of aging.

Making Realism a priority over Aspiration translates for older women into relatable and attainable, both in un-fetishized mature beauty and health; this is not ageless aging. In a way, it respects older women's life experiences as a source of knowing and being in the world. It is a life-course perspective that honors where women are in their journey of aging-well within their age.

Let's finish with 13 Optimal Aging Secrets You Should Know

Mike Waters is a friend and long-time colleague in the field of aging. He is now associated with a new concept in wellness-aging called Fitness Over Fifty. This association affords Mike a rich network of older adults who are living the kind of lives that do justice to what's been called "The Longevity Dividend." This email exchange between Mike and an 80-year-old woman needed to be shared because it hits on so many of the gerontological concepts privileged by those of us working to change the conversation around

136

aging. I will highlight in bold the themes and summarize them.

Please enjoy this content-rich message from someone who is truly aging well and Kicking Butt:

*And Michael, you know I always **like to create new names for transitional stages of life.** After celebrating my 80th, I noticed that there was still a lot of disbelief among classmates and friends about how our "well' bodies could become so 'different'....and that we sometimes felt betrayed by our bodies (reality being that we betrayed our bodies in most instances). We were still doing too much complaining and were deterred by it all at times. By the way, I have 3 years post brain surgery as of today, **still active and also care taking_(name), and my sister and I can celebrate 45 years of being non-smokers.***

*   **But being a curious lifelong learner**, I started calling my 90-year-old friends who are still living fruitful and grateful lives...yet know most of them must have aches, pains, and issues just from the aging process. **Yet, they talked more about life, travel, love and new experiences rather than aches and pains and what they can no longer do.** They said they are so **grateful to have made it to90**that they are through with complaining and fighting the process. **They are in acceptance.** Yet if we are honest, **we all need one friend or family member** that we can gripe, complain and laugh at ourselves every so often...in other words, I still have*

not met a perfect person...guess they all ascended.

*Very non-professional interviewing as I only interviewed non-complainers and women who are lifelong learners. All of them **still enjoy humor and laughter**...Sooooo, my name for living in the 80's stage is "**RENEGOTIATING with SELF into the ACCEPTANCE STAGE**". Example, I still like to **mow my own lawn with a non-propelled mower.** Yet the only area I have arthritis is in my right hand, and holding the mower handle can aggravate it. Since **I now am looking for ways to keep my hands mobile and to continue doing my numerous projects that give me satisfaction and sense of purpose,** I have accepted the fact, and renegotiated with myself that **I will still get to mow the front lawn and delegate the big back yard mowing to professionals or my grandchildren...if I can catch them.***

*With this technique, I can continue to thrive rather than just survive. I remember my mother was told by a few people in Corvallis that 'women don't mow the lawn', but she mowed the lawn into her late 70's and my Dad into his 90's. I laughed when Mom said," **Some people prefer taking medications for anger/stress.... I just mow the lawn".***

***Being retired is great because I can conduct non-scientific studies, say what I want, and still not lose my job!** Will continue to enjoy how you all in the wellness field are renegotiating HOW and WHO you best can serve at this time*

138

in your lives...keep up the purposeful work. Respectfully, (her name).

Summary/Unpack Critical Gerontology Themes

1) **Life-course Perspective**..." *like to create new names for transitional stages of life."*

2) **Activity Theory of Aging** ...*how our "well' bodies could become so 'different'....and that we sometimes felt betrayed by our bodies (reality being that we betrayed our bodies in most instances).* Note she remains active.

3) **Service to Others** ...*still active and also care taking*

_____*(name)*

4) ***Compressing Morbidity** ..." *still active and also care tak- ing_ (name), and my sister and I can celebrate 45 years of being non-smokers."*

5) **Lifelong Learning (staying curious)** ..." *But being a curious lifelong learner..."*

6) **Growth Mindset / Resist Biomedicalization of Aging**..." *Yet, they talked more about life, travel, love and new experiences rather than aches and pains and what they can no longer do."*

7) **Gratitude**..." *grateful to have made it to 90."*

8) **Social Capital**..." *we all need one friend or family*

member..."

9) **Self-Awareness**...*"RENEGOTIATING with SELF into the ACCEPTANCE STAGE."*

10) <u>Environmental Press</u> / **Ecological Theory of Aging**...*"I still like to mow my own lawn with a non-propelled mower."*

11) **Inter-dependence (verses Independence)** ..."*delegate the big back yard mowing to professionals or my grandchildren...if I can catch them."*

12) **Selective Optimization with Compensation Theory**...*"Some people prefer taking medications for anger/stress.... I just mow the lawn."*

13) **Late Freedom Theory** *"Being retired is great because I can conduct non-scientific studies, say what I want, and still not lose my job!"*

This was a remarkable message sent to my colleague Mike Waters. It is a concise and eloquent summation of "Successful Aging" (not ageless aging) and I suggest the readers mindfully read over her words a second time, and incorporate them into your life—for an optimal experience of growing older and Kicking Butt!

(note: Names were left out to facilitate confidentiality)

<u>Final Point on Aging</u>

We have 3 Ages:

1) Chronological Age-Age on your birth certificate

2) Physiological Age-Age of your biology and biomarkers

3) Psychological Age-Age of how you think (fixed mindset or growth mindset)

They are all important, but the psychological age is possibly the key to aging well within all 3 ages (not talking about anti-aging). Successful aging begins first in the mind—then in the physical.

In Conclusion

And so, dear reader, as you close this book, remember aging isn't a problem to solve—it's a plot twist to enjoy. Every stage of life has its perks, and this one's no different. You've earned your stories, your wisdom, and yes, maybe a few extra laughs at things you once took too seriously. Life isn't about clinging to who you were—it's about embracing who you're becoming.

I hope this book has caused you to rethink aging, reimagine your life at this stage, reconsider your self-imposed limitations because of your "age", and reinvigorated your potential for getting older and KICKING BUTT!

Author notes: If you found this book helpful in any way, I 'd so appreciate a review on Amazon. It might just help another person who is getting older and needs KICK in the BUTT!

Reference

*Compressing Morbidity

HEALTHY AGING WAS ONCE thought to be a contradiction in terms. Enter James Fries, a professor of medicine at Stanford University School of Medicine. Early in his career, he foresaw a society in which the active and vital years of life would increase in length, the onset of morbidity would be postponed, and the total amount of lifetime disability would decrease. At the heart of his vision is an emphasis on improvements in preventive medicine and the untapped potential of health promotion and prevention.

Known as "compression of morbidity," Fries' hypothesis holds that if the age at the onset of the first chronic infirmity can be postponed more rapidly than the age of death, then the lifetime illness burden may be compressed into a shorter period of time nearer to the age of death. Evidence supporting this hypothesis thus must take two forms: first, that it is possible to substantially delay the onset of infirmity; second, that the accompanying increases in longevity will be comparatively modest.

Source: Swartz A. James Fries: healthy aging pioneer. Am J Public Health. 2008 Jul;98(7):1163-6. doi: 10.2105/AJPH.2008.135731. Epub 2008 May 29. PMID: 18511711; PMCID: PMC2424092.

Author notes: ***Compressing Morbidity** just means holding off disease until the very end of life. So, most of life is lived in good health, and only at the very end (last few months) does disease take hold.

Friedan, B. (1993). *The fountain of age*. Simon & Schuster.

Gillick, M. R. (2006). *The denial of aging: Perpetual youth, eternal life, and other dangerous fantasies*. Harvard University Press.

About the Author

Patrick spent the first years of his life crawling around the floors of a nursing home where his grandmother was the head nurse. He feels this experience imprinted him and influenced his life's work.

Patrick is an award-winning nurse, his career spanned over 35 years and included ICU, CCU, Trauma, Inner-city Public Health, YMCA Car- diac Therapy Volunteer, and post-surgical recovery. He holds a PhD. Gerontology, MS Adult Education, BSN Nursing, and is a Certified Aging in Place Specialists (CAPS). He is a published author and creator of the website aginginplace.com.

Patrick's Motto: Eat < Move + Purpose + Growth Mindset + Sleep + Aging in Place Design x Community = Healthy Aging Inter-dependence for Life!

You can connect with me on:

🌐 https://aginginplace.com

Subscribe to my newsletter:

✉ https://aginginplace.com

Also, by Patrick Roden

Books by Patrick are all influenced by his philosophy called "Possibility Aging."

The Senior Real Estate Market Advantage: 10 HIGH-Demand Features Today's WEALTHIEST Buyers Desire: Secrets to Forever Homes Sought by the Most Affluent Generation in History

Capitalize on the Booming Senior Real Estate Market by Discovering Insider Secrets to Profitable Opportunities Driven by the Wealthiest Generation in History.

As the wealthiest generation in history, Baby Boomers and GenX control a staggering 72% of the nation's wealth and are redefining their future housing needs.

In **"The Senior Real Estate Market Advantage,"** you'll discover the 10 HIGH-demand features that today's discerning seniors seek in their forever homes. This book reveals key elements that make properties irresistible to these buyers. Filled with ideas this generation wants, and some they don't know exist yet—but once they do, will be highly motivating.

Inside, you'll find:

Insightful Analysis: Understand the desires behind

147

seniors' housing choices and how to align your offerings with their evolving preferences. **Actionable Strategies:** Gain practical tips for integrating high-

demand features into your properties to meet the expectations of this affluent demographic.

Market Trends: Stay ahead with the latest trends and data on senior housing, equipping you for success in a competitive landscape.

Case Studies: Learn from compelling stories of seniors who have successfully navigated their housing journeys, providing inspiration for both buyers and real estate professionals.

Whether you're a realtor, investor, or senior in the market for forever homes, this comprehensive resource will empower you to make savvy decisions in this booming marketplace.

Women, Aging & Myths: 10 Steps to Loving Your Long Life

When you think of becoming an older woman, do your thoughts turn mostly positive or negative?

Why? For many, they turn negative—almost by default. If this is you or someone you know, you might be bound by cultural myths about women's aging. We are aged by biology and culture—especially women. Growing old alone, becoming invisible, dependent, sick, a bag lady, or fearing the uncertainty, are not the inevitable outcomes of living a long life. At least they don't have to be for you.

Many of our views on aging, and women's aging specifically, are simply past myths lingering in a youth-obsessed culture. Only recently have these false narratives been challenged. This book takes on ten myths about women and aging, explores theories, and tells the myth-busting lived experiences of ten women defying them. You will come away inspired and looking forward to loving your long life.

You will learn:

-Why it is not about "anti-aging"

-The Grandmother Hypothesis (no need to be a grandmother) - Why Negative Visualization can support your independence – What Social Capital is and how to leverage it for longevity - -- How decluttering now is an act of love - Why novelty and complexity should be a daily experience as you age A simple technique for reframing aging that will be your new super-power. The components of a systems approach to healthy aging Dreams denied do not have to be, and more . . .

Women find themselves, in this culture, at the apex of ageism and sexism, and for women of color, racism. The underlying theme of this book is "possibility aging," not anti-aging, but aging well within your age and changing cultural myths.

"I had the best year of my life at 80!"

—DeEtte Sauer/U.S. Masters Swimmer

PREjuvenation Influencers: A Mother's Guide to Helping Daughters Break Free from Anti-Aging Beauty Standards

Social media is targeting preteens and tweens with anti-aging content that fuels anxiety and distorts their self-worth. *PREjuvenation Influencers* is a guide that can help mothers counter the negative messaging exploiting anti-aging fears in young girls.

Topics Covered

Understand the Influence: Learn how prejuvenation messaging subtly impacts young girls' perception of beauty and their mental health.

Combat the Fear of Aging: Discover why society's obsession with eternal youth breeds insecurity and how to shift this narrative at home. **Emotional and Psychological Insights**: The hidden psychological tolls of beauty standards on developing self-esteem—and how to address them.

Generational Perspectives: Explore how mothers' own beliefs about aging influence their daughters and practical ways to break the cycle.

Fathers' Role: Insights on engaging fathers to promote a balanced, positive view of beauty and aging.

Expert-Backed Guidance: Strategies and advice from

psychologists, dermatologists, and sociologists to build resilience and healthy self- images.

Practical Tips for Parents: Media literacy, positive role modeling, and curated social media strategies that protect mental health.

Take the first step toward helping your daughter navigate social media prejuvenation culture so she can define "beauty" on her own terms. **Get your copy today.**

Granddaughter, What I Want You to Know About Aging: A Journal for a Granddaughter from a Grandmother

Love leaves clues . . . from a grandmother to a granddaughter. An intergenerational gift and keepsake in the making.

This journal is guided, meaning it is designed with prompt statements that will get your ideas flowing. There are five sections:

Lifespan: Life Experience and Aging Health span: Health Wellness and Aging Soul span: Intangibles of Aging

Section: Aging Secrets You've Learned Bonus: Grandmother's Wisdom Shared

You decide where to begin and what to include. The goal for this journey is to enjoy the process. You have so much life experience, both challenging and rewarding, to share. Take your time, leave your inner critic, write like you're writing to a younger self. If an idea comes to you, jot it down, enter it later, there's no order.

Go away for the weekend with a glass of wine or invite others to help in the process. Create at your own pace, let it evolve into a work of personal expression and love. There is plenty of space to add your own sections. Be creative, be honest with yourself, share freely, include your hopes, dreams, accomplishments, as well as regrets, fears, and disappointments. Themes will emerge about your Aging that may surprise, astonish, reaffirm, or even challenge your thinking. Be authentic to wherever the muse leads you.

It is about you—for your granddaughter. That is the gift. This off-line hard copy journal allows you to control the narrative privately.